Editor-in-Chief and Founder:
  Lyndon H. LaRouche, Jr.
Editorial Board: *Lyndon H. LaRouche, Jr. , Helga Zepp-LaRouche, Paul Gallagher, Tony Papert, Gerald Rose, Dennis Small, Jeffrey Steinberg, William Wertz*
Co-Editors: *Paul Gallagher, Tony Papert*
Managing Editor: *Nancy Spannaus*
Technology: *Marsha Freeman*
Books: *Katherine Notley*
Ebooks: *Richard Burden*
Graphics: *Alan Yue*
Photos: *Stuart Lewis*
Circulation Manager: *Stanley Ezrol*

INTELLIGENCE DIRECTORS
Counterintelligence: *Jeffrey Steinberg, Michele Steinberg*
Economics: *John Hoefle, Marcia Merry Baker, Paul Gallagher*
History: *Anton Chaitkin*
Ibero-America: *Dennis Small*
Russia and Eastern Europe: *Rachel Douglas*
United States: *Debra Freeman*

INTERNATIONAL BUREAUS
Bogotá: *Miriam Redondo*
Berlin: *Rainer Apel*
Copenhagen: *Tom Gillesberg*
Houston: *Harley Schlanger*
Lima: *Sara Madueño*
Melbourne: *Robert Barwick*
Mexico City: *Gerardo Castilleja Chávez*
New Delhi: *Ramtanu Maitra*
Paris: *Christine Bierre*
Stockholm: *Ulf Sandmark*
United Nations, N.Y.C.: *Leni Rubinstein*
Washington, D.C.: *William Jones*
Wiesbaden: *Göran Haglund*

ON THE WEB
e-mail: eirns@larouchepub.com
www.larouchepub.com
www.executiveintelligencereview.com
www.larouchepub.com/eiw
Webmaster: *John Sigerson*
Assistant Webmaster: *George Hollis*
Editor, Arabic-language edition: *Hussein Askary*

EIR (ISSN 0273-6314) *is published weekly (50 issues), by EIR News Service, Inc., P.O. Box 17390, Washington, D.C. 20041-0390.* (703) 777-9451

European Headquarters: E.I.R. GmbH, Postfach Bahnstrasse 9a, D-65205, Wiesbaden, Germany
Tel: 49-611-73650
Homepage: http://www.eirna.com
e-mail: eirna@eirna.com
Director: Georg Neudecker

Montreal, Canada: 514-461-1557

Denmark: EIR - Danmark, Sankt Knuds Vej 11, basement left, DK-1903 Frederiksberg, Denmark.
Tel.: +45 35 43 60 40, Fax: +45 35 43 87 57. e-mail: eirdk@hotmail.com.

Mexico City: EIR, Sor Juana Inés de la Cruz 242-2 Col. Agricultura C.P. 11360 Delegación M. Hidalgo, México D.F.
Tel. (5525) 5318-2301
eirmexico@gmail.com

Canada Post Publication Sales Agreement #40683579

Postmaster: Send all address changes to *EIR*, P.O. Box 17390, Washington, D.C. 20041-0390.

Signed articles in *EIR* represent the views of the authors, and not necessarily those of the Editorial Board.

A Turning Point In History: The Bush Family Takeover Begins

March 30, 1981: The President Is Shot

Oct. 27—The courageous actions of Russia's President Vladimir Putin in the Middle East, have now created a new historical turning point for the world. Thanks to what Putin has done, it is still within the realm of possibility to rescue the human race from the long-ranging policies represented by Obama, which would otherwise exterminate us,—or nearly so.

But the leadership for this last-ditch rescue is strictly limited to those very few (actual) leaders who understand the significance of the previous historical turning-point of March 30, 1981, when President Reagan came close to death by an assassination-attempt by Bush family associate John Hinckley, Jr. That leadership excludes our far more numerous merely-nominal leaders, whose advice will kill us all. That is, all those who are ignorant of the significance of March 30, 1981,—like nearly all our Members of Congress. Even worse are those unfortunates who believe they understand it based on gossip and rumors, but don't.

Even before his election, President Reagan had assigned Lyndon H. LaRouche, Jr., to develop, and later to negotiate policies bearing on security and relations with the Soviets. LaRouche's policy, which he had been elaborating since 1977, was that to which the President later gave the name of the "Strategic Defense Initiative," or SDI. (The late eminent scientist Dr. Edward Teller partnered with LaRouche on this.)

Whatever ignorant fools may say, the SDI was not based on the interests of one nation opposed to others, but on the shared interests of a community of all nations,—what Dr. Teller called "the common aims of mankind." The SDI was an expression of those ideas of Alexander Hamilton which gave birth to the United States before and during George Washington's two terms as President. But yet, even the very political organization Lyndon LaRouche had earlier founded, nevertheless failed to provide such leadership from the moment he went to prison in 1989,—when the terrified members fragmented it into competing, franchise-like local organizations,—until after he began to re-found it as a Manhattan-based, centralized Hamiltonian organization just one year ago.

From 1980 at the latest, the Bush family, acting as protected British agents, had moved to destroy the SDI by attacking first Reagan, then LaRouche. (Attacking both at once would have betrayed their hand.) Reagan's physical toughness enabled him to return to full function within a year after he was shot,—but the intervening period permitted Vice President George H.W. Bush, who had been forced onto Reagan's ticket, to begin a power grab. The long efforts towards a criminal frameup of LaRouche began at the same time. Then, with LaRouche under attack, President Reagan was destabilized. Nevertheless, that President maintained his own personal commitment to the SDI, refusing massive pressure to forswear it, all the way through his two terms in office.

The triumph of LaRouche's SDI policy was on March 23, 1983, when Reagan publicly announced it as U.S. policy and publicly offered it to the Soviets on equal terms, in a nationwide television address. But the British-Bush effort to undermine it was already well-advanced.

Since March 30, 1981, the trajectory of the United States and the Transatlantic sector has been down, down and down.

Amidst the vast destruction wrought by the Bushes and Obama, President Bill Clinton sought to restore the country under a functioning Presidency. He implicitly supported LaRouche's continuing work which continued the SDI policy under new circumstances. But President Clinton was badly weakened by his traitorous Vice President, while his wife Hillary failed to understand the policies at issue. Eventually, Queen Elizabeth II, working through certain leaders of the Republican Party whom she used as her puppets, used phony scandals to eviscerate President Clinton before the end of his second term; it was under those circumstances that he signed the disastrous repeal of Franklin Roosevelt's Glass-Steagall legislation.

All this is written here for you to understand it. To understand it before you are tested on it. Learn quickly!—your final exam may be coming before tomorrow morning!

EIR Contents

www.larouchepub.com Volume 42, Number 43, October 30, 2015

Cover This Week

he scene of the attempted assassination of President Reagan, March 30, 1981

Why Americans Must Now Embrace The Initiatives of Vladimir Putin

by Robert Ingraham

If not for Vladimir Putin's intervention, humanity would be finished.

—Lyndon LaRouche

Oct. 25—Lyndon LaRouche speaks of discontinuities, of interruptions—of critical turning points—which have fundamentally altered the course and the potential directionality of human history, whether for the better or for the worse.

Such a negative turning point took place in the 1980s, when the 1981 attempted assassination of President Reagan, followed by the 1989 jailing of Lyndon LaRouche, destroyed the Reagan-LaRouche initiatives which had threatened to end the Malthusian post-1945 Cold War reign by the British Empire and their allies on Wall Street.

EIRNS/Stuart Lewis

The promise of the 1979-1983 discussions between Lyndon LaRouche and President Ronald Reagan's Presidency has now been revived. Here, LaRouche and Reagan discuss at a 1980 Presidential campaign forum in Concord, New Hampshire.

The subsequent eradication of the Strategic Defense Initiative and the LaRouche-Reagan collaboration did not merely kill the positive promise of those initiatives. Rather, by 1989, with Reagan out of office and LaRouche in prison, the stage was set, beginning with the London-manipulated re-unification of Germany, for a new, far worse escalated phase in the creation of a dictatorial London-centered world empire.

Through the 1990s, every effort was made by the British and her American stooges to economically destroy and subjugate the republics of the former Soviet Union, particularly Russia. The expansion of NATO into Eastern Europe, in violation of earlier promises to the contrary by U.S. and British officials, was intended to terrorize Russian leaders into military submission. With Russia neutralized, China would be alone, isolated as the only strategic force which posed a danger to trans-Atlantic interests.

The successful 1998-2000 British-directed destruction of the Clinton Presidency, the repeal of Glass-Steagall in the United States, and the Sept. 11, 2001 British-Saudi attacks on Manhattan then propelled the world into an "end-game" scenario, in which all opposition to London-Wall Street rule was targeted to be crushed, either through diplomatic, economic or military means. The intention: not simply a "unipolar" world, but a Malthusian, dictatorial London-Wall Street empire. It is this drive for global dictatorship that we have been living through during the past 15 years of the Bush and Obama presidencies.

Vladimir Putin Today

Between Oct. 19 and Oct. 22, a three-day meeting of the Valdai Discussion Club was held in Sochi, Russia, with participants from Russia, Europe, Asia, Africa, the United States, and South America. The topic of this year's event was "Societies Between War and Peace: Overcoming the Logic of Conflict in Tomorrow's

World." The following paragraphs are excerpts from Vladimir Putin's speech to that conference:

We have an open discussion here; this is an open intellectual platform for an exchange of views, assessments and forecasts that are very important for us here in Russia. I would like to thank all the Russian and foreign politicians, experts, public figures and journalists taking part in the work of this club… This year the discussion focuses on issues of war and peace. This topic has clearly been the concern of humanity throughout its history. Back in ancient times, in antiquity people argued about the nature, the causes of conflicts, about the fair and unfair use of force, of whether wars would always accompany the development of civilization, broken only by cease-fires, or would the time come when arguments and conflicts are resolved without war.…

True, peace, a peaceful life, have always been humanity's ideal. State figures, philosophers and lawyers have often come up with models for a peaceful interaction between nations. Various coalitions and alliances declared that their goal was to ensure strong, "lasting" peace as they used to say. However, the problem was that they often turned to war as a way to resolve the accumulated contradictions, while war itself served as a means for establishing new post-war hierarchies in the world. Meanwhile peace, as a state of world politics, has never been stable and did not come of itself. Periods of peace in both European and world history were always based on securing and maintaining the existing balance of forces…

With the appearance of nuclear weapons, it became clear that there could be no winner in a global conflict. There can be only one end—guaranteed mutual destruction…

No Winners in Nuclear War

Today, unfortunately, we have again come across similar situations. Attempts to promote a model of unilateral domination, as I have said on numerous occasions, have led to an imbalance in the system of international law and global regulation, which means there is a threat, and political, economic or military competition may get out of control.

kremlin.ru

Russian President Vladimir Putin addressed the Valdai International Discussion Club in Sochi, Oct. 22, 2015.

What, for instance, could such uncontrolled competition mean for international security? A growing number of regional conflicts, especially in "border" areas, where the interests of major nations or blocs meet. This can also lead to the probable downfall of the system of non-proliferation of weapons of mass destruction (which I also consider to be very dangerous), which, in turn, would result in a new spiral of the arms race.

We have already seen the appearance of the concept of the so-called disarming first strike, including one with the use of high-precision long-range non-nuclear weapons comparable in their effect to nuclear weapons.

The use of the threat of a nuclear missile attack from Iran as an excuse, as we know, has destroyed the fundamental basis of modern international security—the Anti-Ballistic Missile Treaty. The United States has unilaterally seceded from the treaty. Incidentally, today we have resolved the Iranian issue and there is no threat from Iran and never has been, just as we said.

The thing that seemed to have led our American partners to build an anti-missile defense system is gone. It would be reasonable to expect work to develop the U.S. anti-missile defense system to come to an end as well. What is actu-

The so-called Iran threat discredited: Secretary of State John Kerry bids farewell to Iranian Foreign Minister Zarif following the Vienna announcement of the P5+1 agreement on July 14, 2015.

ally happening? Nothing of the kind, or actually the opposite—everything continues...

To put it plainly, they (the Americans) were lying. It was not about the hypothetical Iranian threat, which never existed. It was about an attempt to destroy the strategic balance, to change the balance of forces in their favour not only to dominate, but to have the opportunity to dictate their will to all: to their geopolitical competition and, I believe, to their allies as well. This is a very dangerous scenario, harmful to all, including, in my opinion, to the United States.

The nuclear deterrent lost its value. Some probably even had the illusion that victory of one party in a world conflict was again possible—without irreversible, unacceptable, as experts say, consequences for the winner, if there ever is one.

In the past 25 years, the threshold for the use of force has gone down noticeably. The anti-war immunity we have acquired after two world wars, which we had on a subconscious, psychological level, has become weaker. The very perception of war has changed: for TV viewers it was becoming and has now become an entertaining media picture, as if nobody dies in combat, as if people do not suffer and cities and entire states are not destroyed...

The U.S. Sanctions War

Unfortunately, military terminology is becoming part of everyday life. Thus, trade and sanctions wars have become today's global economic reality—this has become a set phrase used by the media. The sanctions, meanwhile, are often used also as an instrument of unfair competition to put pressure on or completely "throw" competition out of the market. As an example, I could take the outright epidemic of fines imposed on companies, including European ones, by the United States. Flimsy pretexts are being used, and all those who dare violate the unilateral American sanctions are severely punished.

You know, this may not be Russia's business, but this is a discussion club, therefore I will ask: Is that the way one treats allies? No, this is how one treats vassals who dare act as they wish—they are punished for misbehaving.

Last year a fine was imposed on a French bank to a total of almost $9 billion—$8.9 billion, I believe. Toyota paid $1.2 billion, while the German Commerzbank signed an agreement to pay $1.7 billion into the American budget, and so forth.

We also see the development of the process to create non-transparent economic blocs, which is done following practically all the rules of conspiracy. The goal is obvious—to reformat the world economy in a way that would make it possible to extract a greater profit from domination and the spread of economic, trade and technological regulation standards.

The creation of economic blocs by imposing their terms on the strongest players would clearly not make the world safer, but would only create time bombs, conditions for future conflicts...

As you know, our approach is different. While creating the Eurasian Economic Union, we tried to develop relations with our partners, including relations within the Chinese Silk Road Economic Belt initiative. We are actively working on the basis of equality in BRICS, APEC and the G20.

On Syria: The Real Threat to Civilization

We see what is happening in the Middle East. For decades, maybe even centuries, inter-ethnic, religious and political conflicts and acute social issues have been accumulating here. In a word, a storm was brewing there, while attempts to forcefully rearrange the region became the match that led to a real blast, to the destruction of statehood, an outbreak of terrorism and, finally, to growing global risks.

A terrorist organization, the so-called Islamic State, took huge territories under control. Just think about it: if they occupied Damascus or Baghdad, the terrorist gangs could achieve the status of a practically official power, they would create a stronghold for global expansion. Is anyone considering this? It is time the entire international community realized what we are dealing with—it is, in fact, an enemy of civilization and world culture that is bringing with it an ideology of hatred and barbarity, trampling upon morals and world religious values, including those of Islam, thereby compromising it...

We do not need wordplay here; we should not break down the terrorists into moderate and immoderate ones. It would be good to know the difference. Probably, in the opinion of certain experts, it is that the so-called moderate militants behead people in limited numbers or in some delicate fashion.

In actual fact, we now see a real mix of terrorist groups. True, at times militants from the Islamic State, Jabhat al-Nusra, and other Al-Qaeda heirs and splinters, fight each other, but they fight for money, for feeding grounds,—this is what they are fighting for. They are not fighting for ideological reasons, while their essence and methods remain the same: terror, murder, turning people into a timid, frightened, obedient mass.

In the past years the situation has been deteriorating, the terrorists' infrastructure has been growing, along with their numbers, while the weapons provided to the so-called moderate opposition eventually ended up in the hands of terrorist organizations. Moreover, sometimes entire

creative commons/campus of excellence

Martin Blessing, CEO of Commerzbank AG. Commerzbank is the head of one of many European institutions punished by the U.S. for violating sanctions against Russia.

bands would go over to their side, marching in with flying colours, as they say.

Why is it that the efforts of, say, our American partners and their allies in their struggle against the Islamic State have not produced any tangible results? Obviously, this is not about any lack of military equipment or potential. Clearly, the United States has a huge potential, the biggest military potential in the world; only double-crossing is never easy. You declare war on terrorists and simultaneously try to use some of them to arrange the figures on the Middle East board in your own interests, as you may think.

It is impossible to combat terrorism in general if some terrorists are used as a battering ram to overthrow the regimes that are not to one's liking. You cannot get rid of those terrorists; it is only an illusion to think you can get rid of them later, take power away from them, or reach some agreement with them. The situation in Libya is the best example here.

Let us hope that the new government will manage to stabilize the situation, though this is not a fact yet. However, we need to assist in this stabilization...

We currently need to develop a roadmap for the region's economic and social development, to restore basic infrastructure, housing, hospitals and schools. Only this kind of on-site creative

Russian President Putin greets Syrian President Bashar al-Assad in the Kremlin on Oct. 21, 2015.

kremlin.ru

work after eliminating terrorism and reaching a political settlement can stop the enormous flow of refugees to European nations and return those who left to their homelands.

It is clear that Syria will need massive financial, economic and humanitarian assistance in order to heal the wounds of war. We need to determine the format within which we could do this work, getting donor nations and international financial institutions involved...

Syria can become a model for partnership in the name of common interests, resolving problems that affect everyone, and developing an effective risk management system. We already had this opportunity after the end of the Cold War. Unfortunately, we did not take advantage of it. We also had the opportunity in the early 2000s, when Russia, the U.S., and many other nations were faced with terrorist aggression and unfortunately, we were unable to establish a good dynamic for cooperating then, either. I will not return to that and the reasons for why we were unable to do this. I think everyone knows already. Now, what's important is to draw the right lessons from what happened in the past and to move forward...

I am confident that the experience we acquired and today's situation will allow us to finally make the right choice—the choice in favour of cooperation, mutual respect and trust, the choice in favour of peace. [*End excerpts*]

A Moment of Decision

Russia's decision at the end of September to intervene into the Syrian crisis has fundamentally changed the entire world. It has created a new opportunity to escape from the war dynamic of the last fifteen years. This is not about Putin "challenging Obama's leadership," as the lying news media puts it. It is about getting off the road to world war and depopulation. Taking a different path. It is about an opportunity for peace, economic development and friendly cooperation among nations. The mad Obama and his backers are violently opposed to what Putin's Russia is doing because it threatens the very existence of their strategic intentions.

This is not the place for a more in-depth examination of the Putin Presidency, but it should be noted that Vladimir Putin's strategic leadership did not begin with Syria. It can be found in his response to the earlier terrorist attack on Russia, in Chechnya; it can be found in his response to the threat to Russia (and world peace) posed by the expansion of NATO; it can be found in his handling of the Ukraine crisis; it can be found in his role in the creation of the BRICS and the new cooperative economic development policies of that organization.

Now with the intervention into Syria, Putin has upset the strategic apple-cart. He has created a Potential which previously did not exist. Essentially, the promise which existed as a result of the 1979-1983 discussions between Lyndon LaRouche and the national security staff associated with the Reagan Presidency, has now been revived. This is another opportunity—at this very late date—to eliminate the power of London and Wall Street, and to create an entirely new potential for the future of the human race. Once Obama has been removed from office—and for the United States this is an absolute pre-condition—then the United States will be in a position to grasp that potential, to join with Russia, China, India and other friendly nations, and then we will truly have the hope for a new age for mankind.

Only Outside Powers Want To Break Up Syria

Professor Elias Samo teaches International Affairs in Syria and the United States and lectures internationally on the history of the Middle East and the Arab-Israeli Fellow at the National Council on U.S. Arab Relations (NCUSAR) in Washington, D.C. and was Full Professor in the Political Science Department at Central Michigan University for 20 years. Professor Samo taught and helped establish a Graduate Department in International Relations, and established and chaired the Office of International Programs at the University of Aleppo. He also taught International Relations at the University of Kalamoon in Syria.

On Oct. 14, Prof. Samo spoke at the NCUSAR's 24th Annual Arab-U.S. Policymakers Conference in Washington. In his remarks, he said that a great victim in Syria is the truth. He criticized the hypocritical record of regime change pushed by President Barack Obama, and condemned the outside powers, both in the region and in the United States and Western Europe, that have aided and abetted the Islamic and other jihadis. Prof. Samo said that nobody inside Syria wants to break the country up,—that is an outsider's delusion,—and said that it is in the interest of every nation to support Syria's war against the jihadis to keep Syria intact, independent, and sovereign. After the Washington conference, Prof. Samo sat down with EIR's *Jeffrey Steinberg for this interview.*

EIR: I'd like to start with something which you raised at the conference, and raised again just now, which is that inside Syria, there is no desire whatsoever for the country to be broken up.

Samo: Definitely not. No Syrian wants to break up Syria. When I say no Syrian, there's always an exception here and there, but by and large, the Syrians are proud of Syria, are proud of the fact that, as I told you yesterday after the speech at the National Council, Syria is the cradle of civilizations, the home of the monotheistic religions, the home of the two oldest continuously inhabited cities, Damascus and Aleppo.

Syria is mentioned in all the ancient history books and in the Old Testament, the New Testament, and The

creative commons/Disdero

A cradle of ancient civilizations and religions: The shrine of John the Baptist inside the Ummayad mosque's prayer hall in Damascus, Syria.

Quran. Syria is the homeland of Jesus Christ and the first time the term Christianity was used by St. Paul was in Syria. These are things that have value—moral, ethical, civilizational, cultural values that we are proud of. Syria has existed since the beginning. Why would the people of Syria, knowing what they know about their country and the pride they have in it, want to break the country up? There's no way that the Syrians would tell you: Yes, I want to divide my country. The notion of division is being talked about by outsiders.

Proud to Be Syrian

I think most Syrians during the present turmoil have, as I do, two missions:

The first mission is to maintain Syria's sovereignty, unity, and territorial integrity. The second mission is to maintain Eastern Christianity, to maintain the Christians in Syria, because they are the indigenous people. Christians in Syria are the American Indians. Christians in Syria are very loyal, very patriotic. They are the connecting link between the Muslim East and the Christian West. The connecting link between the two cultures, two civilizations.

EIR: One of the things that is really profoundly impressive is that in the Great Mosque in Damascus, right in the middle is the tomb of John the Baptist.

Samo: Yes. Many visitors come to Syria and when they see that, to them it's like when they see a Bishop and a Mufti sitting together in a very friendly, amicable, loving relationship. They take a picture of it. I used to tell groups coming from the West, Europe and America, that Syria is a model for common living. Muslims and Christians living together amicably, in a friendly way, in a very productive way, seeing each other first as human beings, as Syrians, and then in terms of religion, which is not the major factor in the relationship among Syrians of various faiths.

It was exceptional, but a tragedy has hit us, or several tragedies, one of which is, I think, tearing down the social fabric in Syria. There has been a lot of blood between the various components, religious or ethnic Syrians, and it will take a long time for the rift to heal. Nevertheless, despite that, the Syrians still consider themselves as Syrian, as one people.

Hijacked by Islamists

EIR: You mentioned that you traced the troubles back to the fact that what originally started out as the "Arab Spring" became hijacked by some radical Islamists?

Samo: By Islamists, Salafists, yes. It started in late 2010, and then accelerated, snowballed, in 2011 and thereafter in several Arab states. It started as an uprising by people looking for a better life,—employment, good schools, good hospitals, the right to vote, the right to change the leadership, the right to have a say in how they are ruled. This is something very normal, and people rose, asking for these things.

However, with the passage of time, the Arab Spring was kidnapped by the Islamists and Salafists, who turned it into an Islamist Spring, an Arab Fall, and a Christian Winter. The challenge facing the Arabs now is to reclaim their Spring.

When the demonstrations started in Syria in 2011, and turned from peaceful demonstrations to violent demonstrations, the perception in the West—it's an article of faith now—is that it turned into violent demonstrations because the Syrian Forces started firing at the demonstrators. I question that. I question that in the sense that I am not sure who started the violence.

Was it the Syrian Forces who started shooting at the demonstrators, or was it the many sleeper cells who infiltrated the demonstrations and started the violence? It could have been Islamist Salafist cells or Muslim Brotherhood (MB) cells, or Israeli cells or others; and each had its reasons and objectives to ignite the confrontation.

For the MB it was revenge for the beating they took at the hands of the Syrian government during their uprising in the late '70s and early '80s, with the brutal finale in 1982 in the city of Hama. For the Israelis, the demonstrations in 2011 provided the opportunity to deal a blow to Syria to render it an ineffective threat to Israel's security. For the U.S.A. it was an opportunity to destabilize Syria, something they had sought, going back many years. For the Saudis it was both personal and sectarian. The personal had to do with a speech by President Assad prior to 2011 in which he unwisely referred to the Arab leaders as half-men, and for an Arab to be accused of being half a man is the ultimate insult. The second part has to do with the Saudis' desire to have a Sunni ruling authority in Damascus oriented toward the Sunni Arabs, not Shi'ite Iran.

Threats to the Future

EIR: You talked about the greatest threats to the future of Syria. What are those threats? You had mentioned, I think, you said the greatest future threats are that some of the elites have left, including the Christian community, and that over the five years of the war, there are fewer schools, and that the youth without schools will be incapable of operating in a modern economy.

Samo: When I talk about threats to Syria's national security, I talk about Turkey and Israel. Syria is surrounded by Turkey in the north, and Israel in the South, and both occupy Syrian territory. Turkey occupies Alexandretta which was part of Syria, and the French gave it to them, and Israel has occupied the Golan.

Both also would like to have more Syrian territory, and both of them don't wish us well. They've proven that in what Erdogan is doing to Syria now, and the Israelis behind the scenes. So these are the states that threaten our national security.

But what I was talking about that you mentioned—the elite and Christians—is that Syria is going to pay in the future because a substantial number of the elite has left; the economic, industrial, professional elites, the money power, and the brain power have left Syria.

Many of the Christians also are elite; they also have capital power and brain power, and they also have left.

Furthermore, while the present elite deal with the state at the present time, move the state forward now, it is the children who will be the future elite that would lead the country forward, modernize it. Many of the Syrian children have been for the last four or five years without schooling. And not only have we not built new schools that we needed to build, but the schools we had, many of them are destroyed.

We'll have a new generation of Syrians, who have not had access to education.

EIR: Specifically, what is your assessment about two countries? One is Saudi Arabia, where reports are about their help for al-Qaeda in Iraq, which now calls itself Islamic State, and for al-Nusra, funneling a tre-

creative commons/Bernard Gagnon

The thriving commercial quarter of Damascus prior to the assault in 2011.

mendous amount of arms—not just by accident, but deliberately to the Islamists. Do you have a view of what these reports are saying?

Samo: Saudi Arabia is concerned or motivated by fear that the Shi'ite Iranians are establishing a Shi'ite Crescent, extending from Iran to Iraq to Syria, and down to Lebanon. That's their great fear. From a Saudi perspective, there's concern that there's genuinely such a Shi'ite Crescent. But the majority of Syrians are Sunnis, and they have good relations with the Iranians—that does not mean the Syrians will become part of Iran, or part of the Shi'ite Crescent.

I don't think it would ever come to pass that Syria would be part of any Shi'ite Crescent, nor would Lebanon. It's true, the majority of the Iraqis are Shi'ite, but the Sunnis plus Kurds constitute a substantial minority, and they are not going to have a Shi'ite Crescent or control by Iran. I think the Saudis are exaggerating their fear.

EIR: And the Russian situation? It's obviously changed the complexity a great deal.

Samo: I don't know much about military tactics or military strategies, but they are on board. In the final analysis, the Syrian government is recognized by the overwhelming majority of nations in the world. It's a member of the United Nations, and has a government in Damascus. The ruling government in Damascus which represents Syria, has the sovereign right to invite other states to come and help it.

What's wrong with that?

An Epicenter of Crisis

EIR: What would be your best hopes for Syria in the course of the immediate months, and next year or two ahead? What would be, in your view, the best way for Syria to be saved?

Samo: I hope for the survival of Syria and Eastern Christianity. How they come about, how it will work out, I have no crystal ball.

UNICEF

Syrian refugee children at an informal tented school in Lebanon's Bekaa valley in 2013. An entire generation is growing up without access to education.

However, having said that, I am reminded of the proverbial saying, when the elephants fight, the grass suffers. Syria, in particular, and the Fertile Crescent—Syria and Iraq—in general is the fighting ground for six elephants, actually worse than elephants, six brutal historic conflicts which have converged simultaneously on Syria like earthquakes. Syria today is the epicenter, ground zero, of these six crises, and they are:

1) A three-dimensional domestic, regional, and international proxy-war.

a) Domestically, a brutal war pitting the Syrian government against a variety of forces ranging from local warlords, mafias, criminals, to what have become international terrorist organizations such as Daesh and al-Qaida-Nusra in Syria.

b) Regionally, a conflict which includes Turkey, Iran, Saudi Arabia, Qatar, Israel, and others.

c) Internationally, the U.S.A. and some European states vs. Russia. Are we back to the cold war proxy wars of the past Middle Eastern wars? Probably not, hopefully not.

2) Jihad vs. Ijtihad.

It is a historic Islam vs. Islam conflict between the sword and the pen. Jihad was interpreted by some to mean spreading the Islamic faith by force, if necessary, while Ijtihad means to reinterpret and modernize the faith to bring it up to date, taking into consideration time and place. In the present turmoil through the Muslim Arab region, Jihad has raised its ugly head holding the sword in the upper hand, while Ijtihad has lowered its head holding the pen in the lower hand. Jihad is fearless while Ijtihad is fearful, Jihad is moving forward while Ijtihad is dormant. The outcome of this conflict, which goes back to the Tenth Century when it is said that the door for Ijtihad was closed, will have great repercussions on the region and the world.

3) Sunni vs. Shi'a conflict.

This is an old religious divide which traces its origin to the Seventh Century with the rise of Islam.

The conflict originally centered around the legitimate successor Caliph, following the death of Muhammad.

With the passage of time it went beyond the question of succession and developed into theological differences. It went through violent and dormant stages at various historical periods.

Unfortunately, this Sunni-Shi'a conflict has raised its head with vengeance in the Middle East most acutely since the start of the misnamed Arab Spring. The conflict is now being played out in Syria and Iraq, led by

State Department

Potential collaboration? U.S. Secretary of State John Kerry and Russian Foreign Minister Sergey Lavrov shake hands in Geneva on April 17, 2014, after an agreement on Ukraine.

the Sunni, Saudi Arabia, and Turkey on one side and Shi'a Iran on the other.

4) Arabism vs. Salafi Islam.

The Muslim Arab has two primary identities. He is an Arab belonging to the Arab nation and a Muslim belonging to the Muslim nation. When you ask him to prioritize, he will say he is an Arab or a Muslim first.

For the one who prioritizes his Arabism, his Arab nation extends from the Atlantic Ocean to the Persian-Arabian Gulf. He hopes one day the Arab world, which is now divided into 22 states, will unite.

For the Islamist, he sees the whole world a stage for the spread of Islam to engulf the whole world.

5) The historic conflict among Persian, Ottoman, and Arab Empires with the new addition of a fourth potential Judaic Empire. This tripartite ethnic and sectarian conflict has awakened. The protagonists are Iran, Turkey, and the Arabs with a leading role by Saudi Arabia and the stage is Syria and Iraq.

6) The Syrian-Israeli conflict.

Some would say that the biggest instigator and winner in Syria is Israel. A brief explanation of what motivates the present Israeli leadership is the notion of the "Iron Wall" advanced by Jabotinsky in an article written in 1923 titled "The Iron Wall." Its basic premise is that future Israel surrounded by a hostile Muslim Arabs should be protected by an Iron Wall. The first stage of the wall after Israel was created was conventional military power. The second stage of the wall was the development of nuclear power.

The third stage is a strategic wall which is in the making, in which Israel would be surrounded by neutralized or failed Arab States which constitute a threat to Israel: Egypt, Syria and Iraq.

The Egyptian-Israel Peace Treaty neutralized Israel's western frontier. The American invasion of Iraq in 2003 rendered Iraq a fractured, if not a failed, state, which neutralized Israel's Eastern border. Now it is Syria which Israel wants to become a fractured or a failed state, to neutralize its northeast border.

Thus the strategic iron wall would be complete.

Final Reflections

1) Syria, or parts of it, is a swamp full of beasts tearing each other apart in a jungle with no law or order. No nation deserves that.

2) There are four issues regarding Syria: terrorism, Syrian refugees, preserving Syria and the fate of President Assad. In prioritizing these issues, one would think the order would be fighting terrorism, dealing with the flow of Syrian refugees, maintaining Syrian unity, and lastly the fate of President Assad.

There is almost an international consensus on the first three. One would hope that the great influentials would put their act together and deal with these three issues. The fate of President Assad would be determined by the Syrians, not by outsiders. The fall of President Assad now means the fall of Syria.

3) Concerning Eastern Christianity, two bishops were kidnapped in Syria two-and-a-half years ago, Bishop Yohanna Ibrahim of the Syriac Orthodox Church and Bishop Bolos Yazji of the Greek Orthodox Church.

We don't know anything about their fate. Their kidnapping shocked the Syrian Christian community. It was a factor leading to greater Christian emigration from Syria.

Leibniz, Creativity and The World Order

Jason Ross led the discussion with Megan Beets, Benjamin Deniston, and Liona Fan-Chiang on the October 21, 2015 New Paradigm for Mankind show at LaRouche PAC. What follows is an edited transcript.

Jason Ross: The importance of science and of understanding what science is for humanity, is really twofold. One is the importance of making more scientific discoveries, so that we can do more things: developing fusion power, health improvements—there are a lot of discoveries that need to be made, that we need to benefit from.

The other aspect, and the one that I really want to focus on, is how it provides us a better idea for what a basis should be for human relations. How should people relate to each other? How should cultures or nations relate to each other? On what basis can we come together and discuss, what is it that makes us human, a human world?

So the way to do that,—I'm going to use some insights from Gottfried Leibniz, who was really an amazing man, the founder of physical economy. He lived from 1646 to 1716. I'm going to use some insights from him to make some points about what it is to be human, by first setting up some of the problems about how science is presented today, both pop-science, and then also in academic science.

Gottfried Wilhelm Leibniz (1646-1716) considered the unification of efficient and final cause to be among his greatest achievements, of which he had many: in science, industry, statecraft, and theology. This painting was done by Johann Friedrich Wentzel, around 1700.

You could start with education where the discovery process of the past is left out. We get the final discoveries. Students are taught to take tests, rather than to discover new things, and there's little room in that for actual creativity, within the bounds of the official curriculum. You could look at popular representations of science, most of which should make you cringe. But even at their best, even when they don't make horrendous gaffes, they're not providing an insight into how these discoveries really got made. The same problem with education, it's too pat and often it's just misleading. And it certainly does *not* do a good job, or even try, at present, to distinguish what makes our ability to make these discoveries different from what could be done by a computer.

We hear touted all the time what computers are able to do now, and it is wonderful to have increasing automation in a variety of fields. A driver-less car? Sounds great; I'd love to have one. Are computers going to do everything that we can do? And what is it that makes discovery different from everything a computer can do? Who knows? That doesn't get touched on.

Instead, we have reductionism, whereby all concepts are considered as expressible in terms of components parts. I want to look at a couple of aspects of actual science practiced today in this respect, specifically the fields of evolution and of neurobiology. On evolution, let's take, I don't mean to pick on him in particular, but as a good target, look at Dawkins, who's got some notoriety. He wrote the book, *The Selfish Gene*. He wrote the books about why he hates the concept of God. And he's a very strong defender today of what we would call the Darwinian view of evolution, which as explained, where it changes—mostly random changes in DNA, but also other changes, still without a purpose—end up causing changes in organisms from one generation to the next. Some of these changes confer a selective advantage, and those are the ones that end up having more offspring, or kill the other organisms, and do all the mating, or eat more food; those are the organisms that then end up creating the next generations preferentially. So natural selection, slight improvements locally, are what create the evolution that we see over the long scale of hundreds of millions of years in the succession of evolutionary stages.

So what do we make of that? Let's look at two aspects of it. One is the origin of life itself, and the other is, let's take it all the way forward, to the development, the emergence, of human consciousness as an active force on this planet. So as far as we know, there's a certain time before which we haven't found any evidence of life existing on the planet. People hypothesize that life was created on the planet. So people like [Russian biochemist] A.I. Oparin, an enemy of Vernadsky's, said that if you put some simulated lightning and some chemicals together and try to recreate the Hadean Age of the Earth, before there was life, if you just sort of bumble things around, eventually you'll create life, or at least some organic molecules. Now you can do that, and you might make some molecules.[1] No one's ever made life that way.

Take two issues that Vernadsky has with this approach: One, we've never known of just an organism; we've always known only a biosphere. So explaining the origin of life requires more than creating an amino acid or something. How does the biosphere get created? Is it from the beginning of one organism? Well, we haven't ever seen that. He points that out.

The other aspect of it is something about life that distinguishes it from physical and chemical processes,

1. See Meghan Rouillard, "A.I. Oparin: Fraud, Fallacy, or Both?" in *150 Years of Vernadsky: The Biosphere,* published by 21st Century Science & Technology. Available at http://bit.ly/vernadsky-150 and http://21stcenturysciencetech.com/Articles_2013/Spring_2013/Oparin.pdf

FIGURE 1

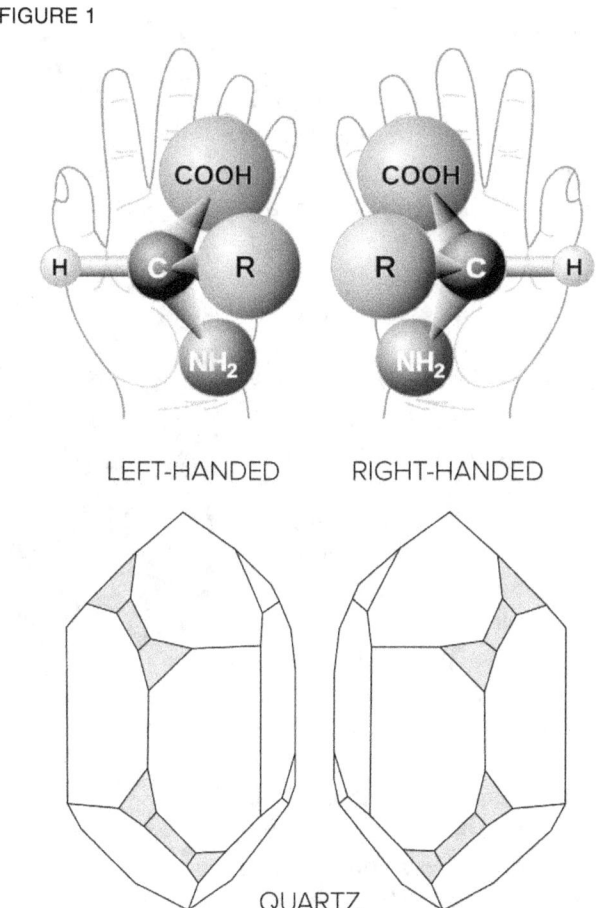

Chirality: Chiral molecules can exist in two forms, differentiated only by being mirror images of each other. Physical and chemical processes are, generally, indifferent to the two types of such stereoisomers, but they are treated totally differently by living processes.

something that had been discovered by Pasteur in [1848]: chirality.[2] Chirality means handedness. Some molecules can exist in two forms that are mirror images of each other, like your two hands. If you talked about which bones and tendons connect to each other, and you wrote it all down, you wouldn't know if you're describing your left hand or your right hand. But they're different. In life they're very different. We find proteins are of one handedness, and carbohydrates or sugars are of a different handedness. Different handednesses of the same molecule smell different to us and have differ-

2. See Vladimir Vernadsky "On the Condition of the Appearance of Life on Earth" in *150 Years of Vernadsky: The Biosphere,* published by *21st Century Science & Technology.* Available at http://bit.ly/vernadsky-150

ent effects on us as medicines.

So how could that ever get created? That's another question to look at. Where did the preference for one hand come from? That's another one, where there are physical or chemical hypotheses to explain it, but nothing that compelling yet. No specific idea why do we have the predominances that we do. Is it chance? Could it be different elsewhere? If there's life on Mars, is it shaped differently? That'd be great to know. Is there something intrinsic about the handedness of life? We just don't know right now.

But that's something that's inexplicable at present from chemical or physical factors. Living processes create one of the two hands, but not the other, or treat them differently, and no purely chemical process does that. And it takes very unusual physical processes to make a distinction.

But let's ask, what else is there to this story of evolution? Vernadsky added more to the story. Vladimir Vernadsky was, if you've been watching our shows, the famous Russian-Ukrainian biogeochemist who did everything. He developed the concepts of the biosphere and the noösphere, where the noösphere is the shaping of the biosphere of the Earth and its surroundings by our minds, by noësis. Vernadsky said, well look, there's more to evolution than this. If we look at what evolution has done, we'll notice a couple of things. One is that the flow of biological compounds, energy, the chemical migrations associated with life. This increases over evolutionary time. Life is becoming more and more active. This *biogeochemical principle* of Vernadsky states that "the biogenic migration of chemical elements in the biosphere tends towards its most complete manifestation." Living matter takes full advantage of the opportunity for activity. The second principle states that "the evolution of species, leading to the creation of new stable, living forms, must move in the direction of an increasing of the biogenic migration of atoms into the biosphere." To Vernadsky, "it is impossible . . . to speak of evolutionary theories without taking

V.I. Vernadsky (1863-1945), the Russian-Ukrainian genius whose great discoveries did not rely on the method of Newton or Laplace, as he remarks in his Study of Life and the New Physics. *This photo is from 1934.*

into account the fundamental question of *the existence of a determined direction, invariable in the process of evolution, in the course of all geological epochs.*" A progression, a direction is seen over evolutionary time, and no theory that does not consider this can be considered complete.[3]

Among organisms, those that contribute towards this process are the ones that evolution has created and developed. They're the ones that exist in increasing numbers. So these biogeochemical principles of evolution that he noted, do those arise from a concept of natural selection itself? No. Unless you operate on faith. Let me read a short quote from Dawkins about his faith on this. He says, "The theory of evolution by cumulative natural selection is the only theory we know of that is in principle *capable* of explaining the existence of organized complexity. Even if the evidence did not favor it, it would *still* be the best theory available."[4]

So what do people do, when they take a reductionist approach? They say we've got a complex process. We have a faith, a certainty, that we could explain it based on the parts that make it up, once we discover what all those parts are, and how they interact. Eventually we'll get there. We're not there yet, but *have faith*. That's what Dawkins says. That's what Oparin says. Now we haven't done it. Right? We haven't explained all of evolution this way. We haven't created life from physical or chemical means. These are open questions.

So, evolution does occur. The Earth isn't only a few thousand years old, but there's more to it then. It's not explained by the Darwin approach, alone.[5]

3. Vernadsky, "The Evolution of Species and Living Matter," translated in *150 Years of Vernadsky: The Noösphere,* published by 21st Century Science Associates, 2014.

4. Richard Dawkins, *The Blind Watchmaker,* 1987.

5. And useful empirical generalizations about the process can be made, without relying on the reductionist approach, as remarked by Vernadsky in his *The Study of Life and the New Physics,* 21st Century Science Associates, 2015.

Let's take a look at another phenomenon, that's a very shocking discontinuity over evolutionary time, and that's us, humankind. We're a shocking change over evolutionary time. And there have been some big shocks. If you were watching the planet, you'd say, OK, life is living in the crust. It's in deep-sea ocean vents munching on sulfur. There's a very limited amount of life that could exist on the planet. There's only so much energy bubbling out of the Earth, these chemicals.

The development of photosynthesis? Wow. That just completely transformed everything. Now the Sun is the source of energy for life, and not just what comes out of the crust. That's a huge change. That's amazing! Oxygen's being created now. Something poisonous. Life had to change to deal with oxygen, which can kill us, too, at high concentrations, at pressure.

Then you move along to get other shocking changes. You have the development of warm-blooded animals; well, first animals, vertebrates, nervous systems, warm-bloodedness, an increasing ability for organisms to create their own environments independent of their surroundings. And then with us, we have the ability to make decisions and act in a way that's independent of our surroundings. Animals are creatures of instinct, and of habit and training when we domesticate them.

Deniston: Hopefully, yes.

Ross: You never know. I think that some people ought to bring their pets when they visit their therapist. They might find some,—I've certainly known some pets who represented definite characteristics of their owners that you would have to be blind not to see. But anyway.

All right, so, we've got consciousness. How does this happen? Is this something that got built up in the pieces? These stupid science magazines every week, they'll talk about how we just discovered the evolutionary advantage of love. Or we just discovered why it's evolutionarily advantageous to have compassion. Because even if you are not related to the person you help, and your gene won't survive into the future, maybe your tribal group, in which you've got a larger correspondence of genes, and outside tribal groups will be benefitted by your altruism towards your, etc. That's called science? Trying to figure out some way of explaining everything this way?

But let's take the mind itself, consciousness. Now, without a doubt, the brain has an impact on our thoughts. There's no doubt about it. At least, definitely on the ability of thought to direct the body. Alzheimer's pa-

tients typically have characteristic structures in the brain that can be seen on scans. Neurosurgeons can identify that there are really things there. And take strokes, for example. Unfortunately, it's a science that really developed through studies of injuries and illnesses, and brain problems. We've been able to piece together, now more recently with MRIs, the different aspects of the different components of the brain, and relationships to various aspects of body, and also characteristics of the mind. Types of memory, certain kinds of feelings in some respects. So there's a connection there, obviously.

People use drugs recreationally. It's not because it makes their feet feel fantastic. I mean these things act on the brain. They create a certain kind of feeling and that's what people are doing it for. Or non-recreationally. So, let's think about this.

Where is the room for free will? It hardly seems like an illusion. Every day we make decisions. We're never surprised that our arms just start doing things that we don't want them to do; typically, for most people, that doesn't happen: When we want to walk, our legs do as we tell them. When we decide what we want to do with ourselves, the body follows. We can choose to think about something, and we can start thinking about it, although we might get distracted. But overall, we've got the ability to determine what we're going to do. Where does that come from, if the brain is biological and chemical?

If we've got that faith that Dawkins and Oparin have, and others, this faith that one day we'll figure it all out from those pieces, where are we in all those pieces? Where is the ability to do something of your choosing? If we are able to say, well, we know how synapses work, we know how neurotransmitters work, we know how a charge is conducted across the body of a nerve cell,—where is our ability to decide what we want to do? How can our thoughts impact something physical, within our bodies, that causes our bodies to do what we have chosen?

It obviously makes much more sense to start from free will, to say clearly this exists. We experience it every day. So a system of thought that wouldn't allow it, just can't be right. But that's not how it goes, if you follow through on the reductionist outlook. By explaining everything from its pieces, really, free will either has to vanish, or it has to be explained as an epiphenomenon, as an emergent property: By combining enough synapses, the synapses are you. Maybe free will is a

Author Jason Ross in the LaRouche PAC video Metaphor: an Intermezzo, *where he explores LaRouche's concept from the standpoint of Kepler. In "The Strategic Situation Now," LaRouche wrote that "Metaphor does not relate to a particular, explicitly direct object, or set of several objects; it refers to an implied simultaneity among a very special quality of several, indirectly related objects."*

little bit of an illusion, but you don't know that it isn't; or perhaps, when you put these things together, thought actually takes place, as a system of these neural structures.

Well, let's take this apart by looking at a very specific aspect of free will. Some aspects of our free will don't seem to differentiate us that much from the animals. You train mice, or they choose which button to push to get some food, or something like that. It seems like they're making decisions. That's not such a profound sense of our free will. What about the free will of doing something that has never been done before, in the specifically human sense of making a discovery? Let's look at that kind of free will, and see if it can be accommodated within an idea of the world that's based purely on those pieces acting in unison, or in concert.

We're going to get to one specific discovery, Leibniz's discovery of *vis viva* [living force], in a little bit. But I want to start with the most general notion of discovery using the concept from LaRouche of metaphor; he says this is the touchstone of understanding what discovery is—metaphor. The process whereby two or more different types of senses, or extended senses through not just using the senses of our body [using scientific instrumentation], where two or more senses are put together in a way that creates a concept that couldn't be derived from anything in the past. It's fundamentally opposed to mathematics, especially to logic. It's some-

thing that's specifically human. So, to give an example of it, and we come to this example a lot, because it is such a prime example; and it's the birth of modern science. It is,—you guessed it! Kepler.

Kepler's discovery of gravitation, of the Solar System as a system, this was an application of metaphor.[6] Before Kepler, astronomers had attempted to understand the motions of the planets as dots in the sky, the stars that moved from night to night, by combining motions of circles upon circles, upon circles, upon circles [epicycles]; depending on the astronomer, the number of circles might differ for was any given planet. And by putting all these circles together, you'd have a model for the motion of the planet. You would calculate where you'd expect to see it, and you'd look and you'd see, is Mars right next to the hip-bone of Leo, or whatever star, where you'd predicted it would be? And that was it. Circles were used because in the heavens, there could be nothing more perfect than the circle. The heavens are perfect, unlike the filthy Earth down here—that was Aristotle's view, which prevailed for quite a long time.

Kepler proved that this mathematical approach couldn't succeed. To make a long story short, he outdid them in what they were trying to do. He made the perfect circle model, or the perfect circle-circle-circle model. He did it, he made a model for Mars with it, it seemed really great; but there was an irreducible, unavoidable, unremovable error of 8 minutes of arc. A minute is 1/60th of a degree. A fraction of a degree of error as to where Mars would be. There's no way to remove it. There was no way of putting those circles together to do any better than a minimum error of eight minutes.

So Kepler says what? This proves to you guys that your approach is wrong. You're trying to just match what we see. You're not asking why they're moving. You've just got these circles. But why are the planets moving? Why are they moving that way? Why are they at those distances? Are you trying to answer any of that? No, you're not. He showed that their approach would never work. He also says, you could always add more

6. See "Metaphor: an Intermezzo" by Jason Ross, at https://youtu.be/aUQUbEoyVoQ

circles, and keep reducing the error. So he said, even if your model matches what you observe, that is *not* proof that you're right. The error might just be too small to observe at this point. If you added a hundred circles, you could match things *really* well. Does that mean that that's how the planets really move? Of course not.

So what Kepler did instead, was to create something totally different. He had a physical principle of gravitation, that the Sun caused the planets to move. It wasn't just sitting in the central seat watching them as a bystander. He had a physical hypothesis. Not only was it not based on mathematics, it couldn't even be expressed in mathematics. The Kepler problem: If you try to express Kepler's principle as to where will a planet be on a certain day, you can't even solve the math for it exactly.[7] So his approach was non-mathematical. It was anti-mathematical: It was physical. It was metaphorical. Even though today we wouldn't accept his physical hypotheses, the specific ones that he was playing with— and he wasn't quite certain about them—we'd definitely see this as a foundation of modern science, where curve fitting is gone, and the discovery of principles corresponding to thoughts in the mind becomes a standard for understanding the world around us.

And it's no surprise that sometimes people today are astonished, that believing, religious people in the past were able to discover great things, as though Kepler's belief in God should have disqualified him from figuring anything out, because God is a terrible delusion that just enslaves and kills people. Some of this atheism stuff gets pretty intense, but it's quite the contrary for Kepler. He viewed human beings as made in the image of God. He said that there's a correspondence between the way our minds work and the way the Universe is composed, such that we'll actually be able to understand it, such that we can ask why. Right? It's possible to ask, *why* is it acting that way, instead of some other way?

And that's not true in every cultural tradition—the idea that that's even a legitimate question. That's certainly not a universal thing. Some cultures would say: You can't know; maybe you could model it, but why it's happening? Who knows? Only God knows that. We don't know that. So keep the importance of Kepler's outlook in mind.

The 1900 Assault on the Mind

Now let's ask, could a computer have done what Kepler did? Let's ask in a general way, can a computer make a discovery? This requires looking at what happened in 1900 briefly, something we've discussed on these shows a few times. As a bare summary of it, and this goes earlier, but just from 1900: In 1900 at a conference of mathematicians, David Hilbert laid out the problem: Is it possible for us to explain all of mathematics, starting with arithmetic, with logic? And maybe we could explain physics, or chemistry, that way too. Let's find out. Is mathematics just a branch of logic?

Now what does logic mean? Logic is a technique for arriving at conclusions from assumptions that you believe are true. What are all the legitimate conclusions you can reach from the assumptions? So logic is about rules for deriving new theorems, as the terminology goes, from your past ones. Start with your axioms. Start with assumptions. Start with your beliefs. What follows from them, using your rules? That's logic. Now things that follow logically, are included [implicitly] in what you already know. Have discoveries, great discoveries, been embedded in what was already thought in the past? It wouldn't be much of a discovery, if you could derive it from what was already known in the past. Discoveries don't happen that way.

Moving forward a bit, we come to Bertrand Russell, who really hated humanity. LaRouche has called him the most evil man of the Twentieth Century, and he's got some tough competition—you might look at some other evil men in the Twentieth Century. So that is quite a statement, to say that Russell is the most evil of them.[8] But he had a *very* all-encompassing goal, and he worked in many fields! He worked in politics. He wanted to nuke the Soviet Union, when we had the bomb and the USSR didn't. He wanted to destroy science.[9] He worked *very hard* on the math project to try to do what Hilbert said, to try to turn all of arithmetic into logic. He invented some new tricks that he pulled from his sleeve to make his system secure from several paradoxes that he knew about. So he went out of his way to make sure that none of these paradoxes could hurt him, that he could

---

7. The "Kepler Problem" relates to an unsolvable expression for the position of a planet at a given time. Attempts to resolve it led to Leibniz's development of the infinitesimal calculus, and Gauss's work on elliptical functions.

8. Lyndon LaRouche, "How Bertrand Russell Became an Evil Man," *Fidelio*, Fall 1994. http://www.schillerinstitute.org/fid_91-96/943a_russell_lhl.html

9. See Jason Ross, "Bertrand Russell, in 1895, Pre-Ordains that the Quantum and Relativity Will Never Be Discovered," at http://larouchepac.nationbuilder.com/riemann_vs_russell

make math logical—until Kurt Gödel proved he was wrong.[10]

Kurt Gödel proved that Russell's dream was impossible. Now, really, Gödel had already known it was impossible, but he proved it. He proved that what Hilbert and Russell were trying to do was a dead end, that there were important concepts, or thoughts, that would not be derivable from the past. This is basically what Gödel showed; that, in other words, there is always more to know, that can't be derived from what happened in the past; even just in arithmetic he showed this was true. There are new important things that you couldn't have gotten from the past, that you can't have a system of logic that's both comprehensive, embracing all possible true things, and free of contradictions. Not possible. And it can't prove of itself, that it knows everything.

So, really, that should have been the end of it; that should have been the end of the idea of artificial intelligence, which should never have gotten off the ground. That really should have been the end of it. It wasn't. What instead happened was that people then said, well, the mind is also subject to this. Yes, maybe we are able to do new things. Maybe we do have free will. Consciousness is an emergent process out of these synapses and neurons, and whatever a computer can do, that's what we're able to do. But nothing else, nothing more. To admit that there is something more the mind could do, would mean that that the build-up of the mind from its components, was wrong. And that they couldn't accept. Because on faith, we're building everything from the pieces.

Let me review what we've talked about so far, and then bring in our friend Leibniz. We've touched on the topic of evolution, of the faith that's expressed by those

Library of Congress (14)

Bertrand Russell (1872-1970), the disgusting racist who later in life proposed threatening the Soviet Union with nuclear attack in order to achieve a last world peace of one world government, got his intellectual start by trying to forbid the practice of creativity.

who say that there is nothing different beyond the pieces, changing, and developing, and combining to represent something higher. We discussed free will, and the impossibility of a purely physical mind, if free will exists. By physical, I mean obeying laws of physics that could be determined from physical processes, and not looking at cognitive ones—not that our *brains* aren't physical. Obviously they're physical; they're not *not* physical.

And then we looked at free will with the specific application of discovery—that application of free will. Is it possible to explain from components, the creation of a discovery of thought, that revolutionizes the vocabulary by which thoughts are considered, and which doesn't follow from the past? And the answer, as proved very completely by Gödel is: No, that's not possible.

Now I want to bring in Leibniz, and see what this man from several centuries ago (again he lived 1646 to 1716), can he add to this discussion. He was a polymath. He did everything. He was involved in science, industry, had his own projects for mining and power transmission, physical power transmission, statecraft, efforts to reunite the churches, and outreach to China, with the idea of embracing the Eurasian continent with the best ideas in the cultures of Europe and China. He said that China and Europe were *not* mutually exclusive concepts, that there was a cultural tradition in China that wasn't totally different from Europe's, which is the approach that some missionaries, or people pushing them, wanted to have. That China is can't be civilized, they're just barbarians, they shouldn't really be treated as human,—Leibniz did not agree with that.

As a young man, he realized that he disagreed with Aristotle, who said that the mind was really a blank slate, on which the pen of experience would write, and that's what fills out our minds.

Leibniz said, no way. There are concepts that are born in the mind, that are not generated from inductive experience from the senses. Induction is the idea that

10. See Jason Ross, "The Failures (and Evil) of Logic: A Particularly Evil Aspect of Bertrand Russell," *EIR* April 4, 2014. Available at: http://www.larouchepub.com/eiw/public/2014/eirv41n14-20140404/56-59_4114.pdf

we observe things of a certain type (of course, even considering things of a certain type is an act of the mind), but we observe these things and we figure out what's common to these observations; we use induction to create a general concept of the observations.

Leibniz said, that's not all there is. Yes, we use our senses, sure, but that doesn't explain everything. There are concepts that just come from the mind itself, that have a valid power in science, in understanding the world around us. He said that this shows, again, that the Creator of the Universe is reflected in the mind of the individual, that human beings are made in the image of God.

At this point, I wanted to talk about one of Leibniz's specific discoveries, that of *vis viva*. I realize that our time is not going to allow it, but it's in the video description. I'll just say something short about it now, and you can watch the full video later.[11] Leibniz, in looking at how motion occurred, at dynamics, moving bodies, and then their power, and looking at mechanics—this is an important field of science—he said that there was something very wrong with Descartes' and Newton's views of this. Descartes said that matter is extension and it's motion. What is stuff? It takes up space, and it moves, in an absolute space. What Leibniz showed, was that the power of a moving body wasn't in anything that you could observe about it; it wasn't its speed. But that you actually had to take its speed squared, and that that represented its power. Now, in summary form, that sounds kind of mathematical, I admit. So I urge people to watch the video, to get the full story behind this.

There's something there besides the motion; there is a power to act that's in matter—there's something real beyond what the senses might induce. And here, I think, is a key concept for us today. Leibniz looked at two different kinds of cause in nature. And, he said—this is using older language—there are efficient causes, moment-to-moment causes; and there are final causes, which is a cause arising from an intention, a goal. If you see your friend in the store holding a jug of milk, and you say, how did you get here? What's going on? The efficient cause would be that his legs moved him into the store, and then his arms picked the milk from the shelves. The final cause would be that your friend wanted to buy some milk, because he has some cookies, or whatever.

---

11. See Jason Ross, *Dynamics and Vis Viva: an Introduction* at http://archive.larouchepac.com/visviva

FIGURE 2

René Descartes (1596-1650) would have been perplexed by a world that actually behaved according to his laws of motion. Leibniz demonstrated that understanding the power of motion is impossible if you are guided by your senses. This depiction from the video Dynamics and Vis Viva: an Introduction at http://archive.larouchepac.com/visviva.

Leibniz said that these aren't exclusive. He said, there's a "kingdom of power," as he called it, by which processes are understood in terms of the moment-to-moment operations, the efficient causes, and that can explain a lot. But there's also a "kingdom of wisdom," which explained, why the efficient causes are as they are. Why are the laws of nature the way they are, instead of another way? Efficient causes can't tell you. But, he said, the "kingdom of wisdom" explains why the efficient causes are the way they are, and very importantly, this kingdom's basis lay in beauty, goodness, or fitness—not just power.

So reductionism, starting from the bottom and growing up—that can never tell us why nature is the way it is, instead of a different way, or why our minds are able to understand it at all. That's almost miraculous, that we can actually understand how nature works. Did it have to be that way? And if it did have to be that way, what was the cause? What kind of cause would that be? *What kind of cause would that be?*

Some people today say, well, if there are a lot of universes, in some of them life couldn't exist, and we're not in one of those, because it's survivor bias, statistically we're in the one that we're in, and there are a lot of other ones out there, somewhere. Not much of an understanding. If you don't conceive,—if you throw away the mind as a cause, you're left with explanations like that.

Let me give one last example of Leibniz's thought, about space and time, and then come back to the beginning. Leibniz corresponded with Samuel Clarke, who was an associate of Newton's. Clarke was a translator of the most popular book on physics, written by a follower of Descartes, Jacques Rohault. In this correspondence, a debate quickly emerged between different concepts of God. Clarke said: God's omnipotent. He can do anything He wants. Leibniz answered, things aren't good because God did them. God did them because they're good. Clarke responded, that means God can't do whatever He wants. He has to be good? Well, what's the point of being God, if you have to be good? Sort of like a would-be dictator. You can see how Clarke's and Newton's view of civil authority reflects their views in this religious idea.

Leibniz said, look, all the qualities that allow of an infinite perfection, all of those are in God. Omnipotence, yes. Also, omniscience. God has to know everything, and be as wise as possible. There's no contradiction in infinite wisdom. So God couldn't do anything without a good reason. Otherwise He wouldn't be infinitely wise. You're only focussing on the power, Clarke, but God is also infinitely wise. That's got to show up.

Clarke said, no way. I'll give you proof. So in the tradition of Descartes and Newton, Clarke said that there's an absolute space and time, like a big shoe-box that surrounds everything. When God decided to create everything, He put it over here in the shoe-box. He could have put everything over there. We wouldn't know the difference. We'd only know how far away the things are that are near us, which would be the same if we're all over here, or all over there; makes no difference. That proves it. God did something without a good reason. That shows how powerful He is.

Leibniz said, the problem is that you assume that space and time existed on their own before God, and that assumption required that He make a choice in putting the

Ferdinand Schmutzer

Albert Einstein (1879-1955) during a Vienna lecture in 1921. Einstein's work subsumed space and time, already shown to be relative by Leibniz, into a single physical space-time concept, and, by uniting energy and mass in $E=mc^2$, had the effect of transforming the meanings of space, time, energy, and matter, in the course of a single decade.

Universe together, that didn't have a good reason for being that way. Therefore, the problem is that you believe in absolute space and time. They don't exist.

That's pretty phenomenal, because this was in the early 1700s, and here is Leibniz using a final cause proof to come to a conclusion about something very physical, space and time. And he was right! There is no absolute space. There is no absolute time. Laws of motion shouldn't differ if you're moving while you're watching motion. This is a principle for Leibniz, and it's a principle for Einstein. Einstein's theory of relativity, built on what Leibniz had done, took that relativity of motion of Leibniz, the non-existence of absolute space, and created something that did away with space and time as separate things altogether—a space-time. Einstein's $E=mc^2$ eliminated the distinction between mass and energy. Now after Einstein, think about it. Space, time, mass, energy, none of these mean what they meant before. Over the period of two decades, these basic terms had their meanings transformed.[12] So that kind of a change, that change in the language, means that you're definitely going to be saying things now, that you couldn't have said before. Right? It's a discovery. It's not expressible in what came before. It doesn't derive from what came before. It's fundamentally new; couldn't be done by a computer, couldn't be done by Bertrand Russell.

I want to wrap up then, going back to my opening concept about the importance of science for the fruits of science—we need fusion power, for example—and for its benefits in understanding humanity in relations among people. We're all human beings. What does that mean? We're all human beings. We've got a shared inheritance of brilliant acts of discovery, of creation—scientific, cultural, musical, political, economic. If we understand that heritage, where it really came from, what it really is, if we hold onto that, and embrace that as our

12. Vernadsky, *The Study of Life and the New Physics.*

humanity, that we recognize to be the basis of our joint humanity, that's a real basis for relations among people and among national cultures.

As Lyndon and Helga LaRouche have said repeatedly and recently, a unipolar world can't exist, but neither can a multipolar world, simply. Right? A new paradigm of human relations has to be forged, based on that ability that's unique to us, not shared with any other form of life, or computers, to create a future that never could have existed yesterday. And on that basis, on the uniqueness of our minds, as being in coherence with the Universe as a whole, we can set a very firm foundation for what relations among nations, and among people, should be.

That's what I wanted to say.

Liona Fan-Chiang: Well, that sets a very high standard.

Ross: [laughs] Yes!

Fan-Chiang: But the other thing is that it sets a higher standard that evolves, so you have a definition of what governs relations among nations, among human beings, and that definition is going to continue to change, based on a basic characteristic of humans, which is discovery.

Vernadsky has a discussion that says, life exists, cognition exists; and it is what you said, but sort of the inverted way, which is, these things exist, and so you can't say that they are not of this Universe. And so, if you are going to say that you have Universal laws, then you must encompass the laws that govern life and cognition. And it's funny, because you said, the mind can't be totally encompassed by laws of physics, at least as it's taught today. But, it really is that the laws of physics just don't encompass the Universe, at this point.

Deniston: I think metaphor is really a good reference point for getting at the importance of these concepts. And Kepler *is* a good example of this: You take his *Harmony of the World,* you take Book 4, what he discusses there, his explicit attack on Aristotle, like you

Frankfurt University's Pictures of Famous Physicists

Johannes Kepler (1571-1630) demonstrated the efficient power of metaphor with his discovery of the Solar System.

were saying, this blank slate idea, that knowledge is just what's presented to the senses and then recorded by the senses and imprinted on you; that's what knowledge is, that's the basis of human action in the Universe. Then you reference Kepler's discovery: It was not just something you got from the senses. It was not something that you took in and observed, but required this action of the mind, this creation of a metaphor. He was great, because he takes *you* through it, too. He writes his whole book recognizing, "well, if readers are going to get this, I'm going to have to take them through how my mind went through the process of figuring it out."

If you went to school and you got Kepler's three laws, his three formulas, you got cheated. You should ask for a refund. It's a lot more fun to read his book and figure out how he thought about what he did; and how he just completely, pedagogically takes the reader, in that day and age, through the way he thought through a process by which he can come to the ironies, the conflicts, which had forced him to come to a new conception. But then, when I was looking at this from the standpoint of Mr. LaRouche's work, I always think it has an extra dimension to it too. Because Mr. LaRouche defines a metric for human progress, human economic advance—the ability of mankind to exist as a greater and greater force in the Universe. And what enables us to do this? It's this unique capability, which you only find in this quality of metaphor. It's this unique capability, demonstrated by Kepler, of the mind generating a new discovery; we see no evidence of animals expressing this capability. And it's that quality of process that is, as far as we can see, the substance of what allows mankind to fundamentally change the way he exists in the Universe; and to exist in the Universe in a completely new way, really, as a function of something the mind generated. Not as of something you observed, not as something Aristotle wrote on his blank slate, but it was something that the mind did, that changed how mankind exists in the Universe.

As you were saying, what does that tell us about Einstein? Einstein said at one point, that the most incomprehensible thing about the Universe is that it is comprehensible, that it's this quality that the mind has uniquely, that allows us to advance, that allows us to make scientific progress. That tells us about the Universe. That comes back on what we can say about what we know the Universe is; that it's that quality of generation of something that the mind can generate uniquely, through this type of process of metaphor, that you're referencing, that's what allows us to exist in a completely new way.

Some of these pop-science people promoting reductionist views—at this point, [they are] people who have just been brought up in this, and they don't really understand the fight anymore. But this is really evil. It's an attempt to kill the actual creative spark that makes mankind unique. This is not just a difference in opinion. This is a direct attack on the idea that mankind has this unique creative principle.

Ross: Yeah, you end up looking at people in terms of their patterns of behavior, instead of their thoughts, for example.

Deniston: Right. The behaviorist school. And you've mentioned how long Aristotle's ideas stuck around, just imprisoning people for centuries in this crazy concept of the mind, and science didn't advance. Mankind didn't advance for centuries, until you had the Renaissance. You just wasted generations upon generations, when people were denied the ability to make some kind of creative contribution to the progress of society, because you had this crazy reductionist dogma imposed on the population. The Twentieth Century has been the beginning of the new phase of that same type of thing.

Fan-Chiang: It wasn't an accident also that Russell attacked metaphor, explicitly, trying to say that valid language, especially a valid language in scientific writing, has to be direct; it has to be exact. It has to be without ambiguity.

Ross: In that it's really not ever going to be new! [laughter]

Fan-Chiang: *And* that it won't be new, and therefore, that it won't be science.

Ross: Yeah. When you said that it's an evolving basis for relations; or think about morality; sometimes, a question people might ask themselves or ask a friend, is whether morality is absolute or is it relative? People, I think, look at that as a question in a wrong way. Absolute sounds like, is it already completed and written

down? In other words, is it done? That's sort of implied in the absolute. The relative meaning, morality's relative, whatever, there's no actual universality to it. Yes, there's an absolute standard of morality, but it's not one that we know yet, and never will completely have known, that the basis for the substance of morality is one that we have to keep discovering, that we do more work on, as we learn more about what it is to be human. So, you think, what's the basis? Why shouldn't I treat people wrong? The Golden Rule, well, because I wouldn't like that to happen to me? Well, that's a good start. Treat people like you'd like to be treated. Well, you should, that's presuming you don't want to mistreat yourself. [laughter]

Deniston: Excluding Dawkins.

Ross: Well, yeah. But why does every human being on this planet deserve respect? Or what's the basis of their dignity? Do we all look the same, in the sense that we walk on two feet, and we don't have a whole lot of hair, and you can tell that we are all human beings? The fact that we're all one species, and that we can all reproduce with each other, and that's what makes us all human, by the definition of an animal species? We can reproduce and have fertile offspring? No! That's not why people are deserving of dignity and respect and a love for and urge to develop them. It's because of this ability that every person on this planet has, the ability in their lifetime to contribute something of enduring value. But how many people in history have done that, or have been in a position to do that? We're really in a position now to end, to really wipe out oligarchism. Things are really coming to a head right now, with the complete collapse of the financial system totally, the incredible opportunity represented by the BRICS. And then the scandal, after scandal, after scandal and attack, after attack, that's all coming down on Obama right now, except at that Democratic debate. But in the real world, he's being slammed from every possible direction. It's a real opportunity to say, "Hey, this has got to go, and instead, here's a real basis for relations among nations."

We have got to develop the world, because people deserve human rights, and you can enumerate them. People have a right to shelter? Yes. People should be able to eat enough? Yes, of course. People should have clean water? Yes, we can all agree on that. Electricity? Yes. Why? What's the basis? And then what's that highest right, to know that when you die, you're not dead? In a real way, to be able to know "I did something; I was able in my life to do something that's going to have

Tsar Peter the Great of Russia (1672-1725)

John Winthrop, Jr. (1606-1676), Governor of Connecticut

Leibniz's scientific and political influence spanned the globe, playing a role in shaping the ideas of great reformers in Russia, the U.S., and China. He advised Peter the Great on establishing the Russian Academy of Sciences; corresponded with John Winthrop, Jr., among other Americans; and provided advice to missionaries going to China, as part of an overall program advocating cultural exchange.

Leibniz's Novissima Sinica (News from China), published in 1697.

kind, is what makes us a species, what makes us unique on this planet.

Ross: We need meaning. We need to give meaning.

Megan Beets: You mentioned that it's just been a very small percentage of all humans who have ever existed, who have acted in this way. I think it's worth letting your imagination work, to envision what it might be like if the majority of humanity acted in the footsteps of genius. What would that mean? What would that do to the physical Universe? How rapidly would that start to transform the physical Universe in a certain unified direction? And it's really an incredible prospect, which is very much at our fingertips right now.

Ross: Yeah. If it was normal for children to think, "Oh, there goes little Einstein and little Marie Curie," and that that was typical, as opposed to unusual, or shocking—imagine.

Beet: Right. And, of course, you'll always have great geniuses who trailblaze and drive that next revolution. But if the majority of the population

meaning beyond it." That's the really human thing that we have to give people. It requires all those other rights,—we need those other prerequisites. We should develop all of them. But we've got to keep in mind where it's really come to head. For example, among the UN Development Goals, which say: We're going to reduce poverty, we're going to get rid of this disease. We got rid of smallpox. It should be, *immortality, in the real sense.* That would be a fantastic UN Development Goal.

Deniston: Yes, right. I think that's a demand we're at right now. We have to realize, our existence as man-

could be brought to the standard, where they're living a life which has an impact after them, because they've actually changed the meaning of humanity in some way....

Ross: And with that kind of culture, you could never have had Obama. Or Bush, or the list goes on.

Fan-Chiang: Not as President!

Deniston: I think that probably defines an appropriate challenge for people to think about.

Ross: And to respond to.

Outgrowing the Childhood of Mankind

This is an edited transcript of Lyndon LaRouche's Dialogue with the Manhattan Project of Saturday, October 24.

Dennis Speed: My name is Dennis Speed, and on behalf of the LaRouche Political Action Committee, I want to welcome everybody here.

We seem to be maturing: We seem to have some new process going on which I know Lyn has been talking about. Of course, it was only a couple of weeks ago, that he began discussing this idea of a Manhattan Party, and we seem to be having a lot more fun in Manhattan, so I'd like to first ask Lyn to give us an opening statement, and then we'll go right into questions.

Lyndon LaRouche: Okay, well, it's fairly simple. Manhattan is a very important area in the history of the United States. Without what was done there in our part of the world. We have an excellent opportunity now to provide a keystone for leadership, in terms of the entire consolidation of our population. So, the point is such that we now have a new level of access to the role of the United States as an organization. And I think this has become fairly evident. And I would suggest that, because you know what our routine has been here in this location, that we just simply start.

So that's where we are. We are now, in this sense, using Manhattan as a place from which to organize the necessary steps for our purpose inside the United States, and for what goes beyond that.

And, as I wind up, we'll just go take this thing and start to go with it with the question and answer with me, and it'll all resonate better that way.

Speed: All right, I got it, Lyn. Let's just make sure that the thing is sufficient. So let's go right into questions and answers, and whoever we have first, please come right up.

The Southern Strategy

Q: I want to ask about Jeremy Corbyn. My recollection is that you said that he was for Glass-Steagall and to depose the Queen. Following his election [as British Labour Party head], there was a lot of protest about him. They were calling him a socialist, and they had this to say against him. Were these people saying that because they were frightened of what it is that he has to offer?

Also I got the impression that with his winning, and with his moving into a position of importance, that

---

> **If you cannot create a better Solar System, then what are you doing being human? And that's the point; everything about your life has to be a progressive process of development of the powers of thought and creativity of mankind. There's no other species that I know of that can meet that challenge.**

Scotland would again have their vote to create their own sovereignty. So, would you go into a further explanation and clarify that for me? And as of the moment, what has he done to bring about what would help us to remove ourselves from the control of London?

LaRouche: Well, the point is, London and the British system has been disintegrating. The Queen and the concert around her are now a piece of garbage, essentially. They merely are trying to fill in the cracks. And the British Empire is no longer the British Empire. It's lost that kind of quality of operation. We have new kinds of considerations, but this process is rather complex, because most of the nations in the trans-Atlantic region do not know where they're coming and going. They've lost their sense of identity, and therefore they are very confused. They stab at this and they stab at that.

So I think the best thing to do, to go with this idea—

Destination Manhattan: Immigrants arriving at Ellis Island in New York harbor in the early Twentieth Century.

look, we have a position here in Manhattan: This point in Manhattan is the proper point of reference for the organization of our organization as a whole, and for the whole system of the planet. Now, we have—China's very important; India's very important, other parts of the world are very important. But the problem is the United States. The United States has to be restored to what would be a competent tradition. We've had very little in that. We've had Bushes, and the Bushes are not much good, or they're less than no good. We have all kinds of things which have gone on so far, since the time of Bill Clinton in particular.

But also earlier, where I was involved in the organization, under Reagan, of running up the economy. And then, Reagan got knocked out because they tried to kill him; and didn't quite succeed. And the second thing was, the effect was, that I was put in a tough situation. And so, since that time, except for Bill Clinton, there has been nothing worth talking about in terms of the United States, in terms of its functions.

So we're now a damaged organization, the United States is a damaged organization from that time on. Bill Clinton made some beautiful contributions, but they were not really that strenuous; his wife didn't help him much; she rather put him in another direction, and she's still doing it, and it's getting worse all the time. But that's another question.

So the point is, we now have a situation that we have to recognize,—that we have to stop this stuff about looking at local areas of the United States. Forget it! The United States has one locality, and that is, the United States itself! And when you try to divide the United States into localities as such, you find you're making a mess of everything, and that's what's destroyed the United States in its ability to function.

The history of the United States shows that, with all the problems of the history of the United States, all the fluctuations, and all the damage that has been done. So therefore, the idea that you have to have is a *United* States, not a collection of localities.

Now, it happens to be no coincidence that Manhattan is a very important and leading part of this whole process. And it was done by Alexander Hamilton. And he was the one who organized the organization of the United States, and then, of course, people assassinated him, and that led to a lot of confusion in terms of the history of the United States, because you had four terms of the Presidency after that point, and it was a screwball operation. We've had great Presidents in a few cases, we've had an organization in a few cases.

But we've also had the Southern policy, and the Southern policy in the United States is what has destroyed the United States' capability of functioning. Therefore, we have to return to that commitment, and that's where we stand. And you have to understand the importance of Manhattan. You know, I went to work on this thing, beginning last October, and I said we have to orient to a Manhattan orientation, *not* local orientations. And it's when you take the Manhattan area, and you make it a point of mobilization of our mission, you find that the characteristics of our citizens in Manhattan become quite useful. Because it's only at that point, when we create a unification of our United States, as a *United* States; and when we understand what we mean by that, then you understand,—well, it's not Manhattan, but it's Manhattan in its role as being the unifying point of reference established by Alexander Hamilton. That's the issue. And if you don't have that kind of coherence, you do not have a United States which is capable of functioning reasonably.

Speed: Hmm! Interesting.

A Sudden Change in Identity

Q: [follow-up] I'd like to extend the question. As I understand it, London does still have some control, certainly over Obama, and they are working to try to fortify him and to regain some of his strength. I also had understood that with Corbyn winning the position that he did, that it would probably bring down the Parliament and cause another election, and that he would probably win leadership of the Parliament. If that does happen, does that quicken our position in our country to return ourselves to a better position?

LaRouche: Well, the fact that Corbyn was able to go as far as he has gone so far in his success, is a very important point. The British Empire is now a disintegrated wreck! And the leading figures in that empire are actually scrambled. The Queen doesn't function any more; she has lost the fruit salad of her brains or whatever. The family as a whole is screwed completely. It's a wasteland.

And you have Scotland, which is a peculiar place. I don't know what to say about Scotland; I know I have my family ancestry from Scotland which is fairly impressive. They played a key role in terms of the wars that the United States has sometimes fought, and so forth. But the problem here is that we don't have an institution in Britain which is worth a damn, except for these people who suddenly come up and said "now we're going to take over the leadership of Britain." And that works, in a certain way. It's insecure.

But we have to look at the planet as a whole rather than any part of the locality. It's integral. For example, China: The role of China is the largest role in the planet right now.

What you're going to have to do is go through a sudden change in identity. Let me qualify that precisely to make absolutely sure that you understand what I'm saying. The problem is that we look in terms of particular nations; we say, "this nation, that nation" and so

creative commons/scorpions and centaurs

Zombies of the dying British Empire: Queen Elizabeth and Prince Philip on April 29, 2011.

forth. Now, the function of nations as an assembly of nations, does have a significance, but the problem is that mankind has to effect a unity, a unity of the population of mankind. The unity is largely located in, of course, what we have on planet Earth; but that is not the limit of mankind's role or destiny. There is also the Galaxy; there are also the other parts of the nearby space. These are integral parts of the same thing that includes the United States.

The peculiarity is, of course, in the people of the United States, the people of the Hamilton types of claims,—the types of what people are, in terms of what mankind can become; and that's the issue. You have to think that if mankind is not becoming an increasingly effective force in order of magnitude and quality, and mankind is not achieving things that mankind has never achieved before, then you don't have a competent mankind. Because mankind has a special [mission].

For example, there is no such thing as a particular population being the be-all and end-all of mankind, none. Mankind actually belongs to the Solar System and beyond. And as mankind progresses, we'll find that mankind always is, when he's successful,—mankind always achieves goals which no other species in the Solar System or anywhere could achieve. Mankind's progress in the sense of,—not science as most people talk about it, but the principles of creativity; where the individual people inside society are able to understand and comprehend like our greatest thinkers do, like Vernadsky and people like that; they created a new level of knowledge for the entire human species.

It's that quality of creativity which we must instill in our population. And the meaning of the nation is that the nation has to be a unit,—our nation, our United States, has to be a unit of creativity, permeating the planet as a whole; man's role in the planet as a whole. And if we don't do that, we are not going to succeed; we'd be failures.

The British System is Dying

I mean, the division of the United States, the Southern vs. Northern population, this is a disease. This is not an option, this is a disease. We still have in the Southern parts of the United States, you have a state of evil, which dominates that part of the United States. You have other areas of incompetence; we have areas where we've lost the ability to create and to provide for progress.

Now, the time has come, that we have to look at these things in terms of a total picture; we have to situate the whole experience of mankind on this planet—but also beyond this planet as such. And mankind has to reach out to become capable of mastering points of space and time, which mankind has never been able to master previously. We have to locate the nature of mankind.

And your point that you stated right now, it's valid; yeah, sure it's valid. And what it means is that people like Corbyn and so forth, are actually probably the on-coming of something that is better than Britain has known itself. Maybe a few of my Scottish ancestors have done pretty well; but that's not the big issue.

Q: Thank you very much.

Q: Hi Lyn. It's A— here in New York. We have, in the recent period, been going after the Brits pretty straightforwardly; and we see an effect with that. The Mervyn King of two weeks ago, [former Governor of] the Bank of England; Geithner, an extension of the British earlier this week. And we think that getting a little paranoia into these folks, where they can't just mosey into town and run their mouths, is very useful; because they're hearing voices.

Now, South Africa earlier this week came out very clearly on the subject of CO_2 and what they're expected to do with this Paris conference approaching rapidly. And their response was that it was the equivalent to apartheid; so, they've gone and taken a step in naming

and identifying who the enemy is. As this conference approaches and we continue to organize, how should we take advantage of that type of attack or open rebellion against the British?

LaRouche: I don't think we want to look at it that way. For example, the British system is now in a process of dying; and hopefully, it will never come back. It will never resume. The world is not going to work on the basis of nations as such. Yes, nations have a function, because there are people who have different cultural development and experiences; so you have to take these into account.

But we're headed in a direction where mankind,—when people learn to understand languages better, you're not going to have much of this so-called language division. It will pass over. Because we're so stuck with the tradition of the previous century and of the Twentieth Century itself, we're so stuck with admiration of the peculiarities of that period of time. And we don't realize what's happening. It's not an even development, but it's an essential one.

We are no longer going to be operating on pitting nations against nations, in terms of competition. We have now entered the beginning of the process where, if we are successful, we will actually go through a process; we will have elements of cultural consistency, but we are going to come closer, and closer, and closer to the principles which govern *over* the particular nations. The nations are going to become absorbed, as the nations grow up, and they don't act like little children playing toys any more.

And our job is to help mankind, not to play with little boys' toys any more. It will be a process of growing up; it will be a process which is the highest rate of the development of scientific progress. But it will be that kind of scientific progress which will determine or pre-determine the options of mankind for mankind's future in the Solar System and beyond it; including the Galaxy; or the Galax*ies*.

Q: Hi, Mr. LaRouche. This is R— from Bergen County, New Jersey. It's been one week since the Drone Report revelations came out on *The Intercept* website; and to my knowledge, there hasn't been any major movement in Congress to do something about it, whether that means opening up a major investigation, or a criminal investigation or criminal indictments for these war crimes that are being perpetrated or carried out from the top levels of leadership in the

United States. And I find this to be shocking and outrageous, that our Congress seems to have done absolutely nothing.

What's Wrong with Us?

At least, in watching last night's Friday webcast, which was excellent also, I didn't pick up anything from there. There might be a little bit of movement from the ACLU and maybe some outside organizations who apparently are going to pursue this. But as an American citizen, I am totally disgusted that the Congress has done nothing. They should have been on top of this; they should have been chasing this. They should have been opening up investigations; there should have been criminal indictments. This is hard-core evidence. Therefore, I'm going to say that this government does not have my consent.

LaRouche: That's a reasonable argument. [laughter]

Q: [follow-up] And I want to go further than that. And although I haven't taken a survey, I feel pretty confident that if we were to ask most Americans—most of whom are decent people—whether the government had their consent for their government to play the role of God and decide who is going to live and who is going to die; most Americans would not agree with that. Therefore, I feel fairly confident in saying that this government does not have the consent of the American people. Do you have any comments on that?

LaRouche: Yes. There was no intention to give that kind of consent from the people of the United States. And most of the people in the United States no longer believe that they have an option in this matter; they see themselves largely as victims.

Look at what's happening to the population here. The entire association of the people of the United States is in a process of, mainly, degeneration! The people who had jobs, for example, have a poorer quality of job experience and options. Every year, there's a qualitative degeneration in the conditions of life of the great majority of the people in the United States. Now, we have a concern in this matter—not to use the Quaker language—but actually we can use the term "concern." Some of us fell into that habit, but it's not our fault; it was done to us, we didn't do it.

But the point is, we've got a situation where we actually have to take charge. We have to get rid of Obama; we have to get rid of two terms of Bushes, and you know, the Bushes were not good things to have. Bush-

EIRNS/Stuart Lewis

Father of the Nation: George Washington, as depicted by the sculptor Jean-Antoine Houdon. The statue is in the Richmond, Virginia Capitol building.

league people; not good at all.

So therefore, we don't have the authority of our own Constitution! It has been taken away from us. And this process of degeneration began with the Twentieth Century; it came with people like Bertrand Russell and people of that type. They destroyed the people and the *minds* of the people of the United States to a very large degree. So therefore what we have to do, is we have to have a new school of education. And that is possible; there's all the evidence available. It's on the table; it can be used and discussed and so forth. But we're going to have to have a change in mood; we're going to have to clean up the United States itself.

Now, you've got a mess in Europe. Germany has a certain degree of quality, but it doesn't function; it doesn't function any more. The French don't know what history is any more, they lost it; they threw it away. It wasn't just—well, I could go through that story, but that's another part of the thing.

But the point is that what we have is the leading influences for the good are located in places like Russia; Russia in particular, under Putin. Then you look at what China is doing, under China's leadership. You see what's happening now with India. You're seeing smaller nations who are beginning to pull themselves together, and find an international coalition of trying to work together.

Where this thing is going to lead to if it's successful, is we're going to actually learn to use languages in a different way than we have before; a lot of talent will be developed in a different way. We will be pursuing scientific researches which are not known to practically anybody on this planet right now. The elements of that evidence are there, but very few people in the United States or anywhere else on the planet know very much about this whole thing. They don't have a guidepost for how to do it.

What we have to do, is take the negative approach, and say, "Look, what's wrong with us?" Say in the United States, in particular, and other nations as well. "What's wrong with us? Why do we keep doing things which are absolutely incompetent? Why do we do it? Because we try to adapt ourselves to popular opinion, various varieties of popular opinion?"

The Role of the Teacher

And we've lost the sense of the Columbus principle. Remember Christopher Columbus, who integrated the single planet Earth for a time; did a pretty good job of that. And he was a courageous person. And he did launch, in his period of work, he did launch a new way of thinking about mankind; contrary to kind of European system and related systems which functioned at that time. And Columbus was not just a discoverer; he was a maker of discoveries, of human discoveries.

And we've come to a time now where we're going to go back not to Columbus, but we're going to take the example of what Columbus did, and we're going to recognize that mankind is not based on nations as such. Mankind is based on mankind; and mankind has to discover what mankind is. And the problem today, is very few among mankind know that mankind really means.

And I think what you're contributing to, in your several repeated interventions, *you're* doing it; you are demanding a change in the way that the nation is considered. To make it more rational, more constructive—an obligation to be more constructive in the truest and highest sense. And that's what's important. And I would hope that what we're doing here, on this particular occasion and similar occasions about the world, we would be able to see ourselves as, shall we say, my Scottish ancestors put it: "To see oursels as ithers see us." [Robbie Burns]

Q: Good afternoon. This is J— from Brooklyn New York. I wanted to say something that you may or may not have heard about, but I'd like to get some input from you, because it's really important to me to see what your ideas are about this. Now, as everyone here knows, I'm a teacher. I teach science in middle school; which is 11-, 12-, and 13-year olds. Now, I have always said that Glass-Steagall relates to every single thing in our life that is important. That because of the takedown of Glass-Steagall, we have seen and we are seeing the disintegration of major, necessary institutions; such as our manufacturing, our hospitals, and our schools.

Now, I just want to zero in on the schools a little bit. Recently, there has been a class action suit on attacks by the bureaucracy on teachers. The teacher in question that I'm talking about, I think it was Oct. 16, something like that recent, has filed a class-action suit against the L.A. school system.

Now, this teacher was fired for misconduct; however, the particulars of this so-called "misconduct" are just surrounded by discrepancies and innuendos. So, nobody knows what this "misconduct" was actually about. But what we do know about this teacher is that he had been teaching for over 20 years; he was tenured. He has been an instrumental part of re-establishing Shakespeare, and Classical poetry, and Classical literature in the high school that he was in. And he actually received the Teacher of the Year Award during the last part of the Bush Administration. He was given honors for being the Teacher of the Year; and then just recently, he was fired for misconduct.

What Mankind Means

Well, this brings to mind things that are happening right here in New York City. Our teachers are under attack here in New York City, and from what I can see, all over the United States. And we're under attack because those of us who tell the truth, and who want to make sure that our students are actually taught something, and want to see an end to the miserable dumbing-down of the population and the ending of the lives of our students—who are our future—we are under attack.

I have 20 years in the system; I'm a tenured teacher. I said in my school when a principal came in who was a total demon and who wanted to close us down; I said that she was a closer, and she said that I was insubordinate. And I was; still am. [laughter]

So, I was brought up on some vague charges, just like this young man; and I was suspended for a month without pay, and I was told I needed teacher development. Professional development, because I was "unprofessional" and some of what I was saying to my students about Newton being a fraud, and the need for nuclear energy, and climate change and global warming being ridiculous, I guess that falls under "misconduct." So, I understand this class action suit. As a matter of fact, I'm trying my best to find out how to become a part of it.

And I'd like your comment on that, because we need to end the dumbing-down of our children; we need to teach them the truth. And that's the long, tall, and short of it. Thank you. [applause]

LaRouche: In reply, I would emphasize the following: That we have the ability intrinsically in us, but not much in our practice, of developing the concept of what mankind means; or what it should mean. And the meaning, is that everyone who lives as a human being will die; every human being as of now—and there are no exceptions available to my information now on that— that we die.

Now, what is the meaning of the death of people who die of, shall we say, natural causes; as opposed to the radical kinds of things that sometimes occur also? But in the normal course of society, what is the meaning of death for a senior person, or a person who has been run down because of other reasons as well? What's the meaning? The meaning is that we have to, as a human species, we have to get out from this just plain old gossip idea, of what's going on with us; and realize that mankind, *all mankind* so far, to the best of our knowledge, *dies*.

Now that idea of death is not a tragedy. Because under all kinds of conditions, it is possible for human beings, human individuals, to make a contribution to the advancement of mankind beyond anything that mankind has mastered previously. In other words, the creative powers of the human mind, the ability of the human mind to develop the discovery of things which had never been understood before; and thus, mankind is able to change the character of the Solar System; to change the elements of space and time. Mankind alone can do that; and no one else so far known, can.

And unfortunately, because of the educational systems, and because of the oligarchies and so forth that have been running around, the average person has no active comprehension of what it is to be a human being! Because they accept death as finality; when a true human being, who knows what I know at least, will say, "No, that's not true."

So therefore, the question here, is the idea of progress.

Now, what you have presented here in your report on the misconduct being against you, is just exactly that! Now, I know what you do; I have enough knowledge about what you do from various sources, particularly in these premises. And I know what you do. Now, I actually would like to introduce some additional considerations, but I'm not going to protest against what your considerations are so far; because I know that you're doing very well. And you're doing it in the location which generally are rare areas in terms of quality of education. Manhattan has produced some of the finest products of education of people; and this has been a characteristic which was introduced into Manhattan by the reforms of the educational system.

And so the problem here, is we assume that the death of a human individual is a finality. It should not be a finality; what it should be, is that every human being should be enabled, to develop a mastery of domains of mankind's behavior, which mankind has never achieved before. And therefore, that's the principle of mankind; and no other species that we know of has been able to do that, to meet that challenge. If you cannot create a better Solar System, then what are you doing being human? And that's the point; is that everything about your life has to be a progressive process of development of the powers of thought and creativity of mankind. There's no other species that I know of that can meet that challenge.

> **What's true is the ability of the individual and society to create a state of progress in the condition of development of mankind, which has never been superseded before. And it's the ability to supersede the past, all generations. So that a new baby, a new born person, is potentially, should be, a person who is going to create something by man, and for man, which has never been done before.**

The Challenge in South America

And unfortunately, because of the educational systems, and because of the oligarchies and so forth that have been running around, the average person has no active comprehension of what it is to be a human being! Because they accept death as finality; when a true human being, who knows what I know at least, will say, "No, that's not true."

What's true is the ability of the individual and society to create a state of progress in the condition of development of mankind, which has never been superseded before. And it's the ability to supersede the past, all generations. So that a new baby, a new born person, is potentially, should be, a person who is going to create something by man, and for man, which has never been done before.

In other words, it is the creative process, where mankind creates in mankind, the ability to understand and master knowledge which mankind has never known before. And that is the issue. That's the principle, that is the moral principle.

And therefore, like this young lady here, who just... the same thing. What's a teacher doing, a good teacher doing? A good teacher is trying to, always, day after day after day after day, to take a bunch of children, of young people and these children, to inspire them to know something they didn't know yesterday, which is necessary for them to progress in terms of their aptitudes.

And therefore, we just have to say that we know that experience of educating people, of educating in good schools, progress of mankind, that people become capable as society of what mankind have not been able to do before. But we have to take it further. We have to say mankind's mission, is to create the power of creativity in that way. That the job is to, as any good teacher, like, you know,—you have to educate the people, the students, you have to educate people around you. And you do the best you can in order to advance these children and others, similar other people. You're trying to get them to go a step further than mankind has gone before,

or at least in that institution or in a similar location. The discovery of what is new, the discovery of the original, which is necessary.

And that's the issue. We have to create in ourselves, among our species, we have to change everything we are doing so far. We have to change it. Not because we hate it, but we have to do it because we've got to know something we didn't know up to now.

Q. Good afternoon, Mr. LaRouche. I'm P— from the Bronx, I was born in Guatemala. So today, I attended a meeting with Peruvian officials; they were talking about Peruvian issues. But I spoke privately and also during the event, and I raised questions about joining the BRICS, and the need to focus on the new frontiers in space research and scientific breakthroughs in nuclear energy and other technologies, such as magnetic levitated trains, in order to solve poverty problems. I told them about the developments in Bolivia, about science cities, education for young people, and their commitment to become a nuclear nation.

It was interesting, because there were all kinds of people in the event. There were the greenies, there were the British with British accents, asking about open markets, free markets, or—I don't know! He was the CEO or something. Also there was a beauty queen, who was a former Miss Ghana. And also, a guy with a smart phone, who was all the time looking at the smart phone. So it was very interesting.

But the Peruvian officials, they were really impressed when I spoke to them about your ideas about the technology, and even talked to them about Classical music, and the relationship between Classical music and science, and even gave them some beautiful pictures from NASA, and how everything can be changed, and how to develop the human resources. They were really impressed with that. And then at the end, they asked me, "How can we join the BRICS?" And they praised the BRICS, and they praised what Evo Morales in Bolivia is doing. So it was very nice, it was fun. Thank you.

In other words, it is the creative process, where mankind creates in mankind the ability to understand and master knowledge which mankind has never known before. And that is the issue. That's the principle, that is the moral principle.

Mankind Must Grow Up

LaRouche: OK! What we have to understand is that you're talking about a different part of the Americas, in terms of culture, the implications of that. Well, this is all valid, there's no question about it; it's all valid. The question is, are we making the kind of progress which mankind requires in society? How can we deal with these issues of progress, for example, like different parts of South America, and the culture is somewhat different? It's not really different, however.

And our objective is that we intend that we should not have a reduction of the abilities of different parts of the nations of South America, for example; that there should be a common,—even though the language is different, and the use of the language may have differences; and the cultural history is somewhat different,—the important thing is to recognize mankind.

And therefore, the thing you have to turn to is not the success of some part of the culture of mankind, but of mankind as such. And now you take any of the parts of South America, for example, those that are respectable in terms of their progress,—what do you want to do? You want to bring about a conception of the mind, of the human mind, which fits all cases up to the point of current progress and development. It's that simple.

We're coming to the end of the national system, the idea of different nations. We're coming to the end of that kind of culture. You will see that's happening already; you see it's happening in the effect of China; you see what's happening now, again, with India, new developments in India; you're seeing it throughout the process: Mankind is not divided by special cultures. It is not divided by mankind, it *should* not be divided by mankind! It should be a process of convergence of the human species as a whole, into the new and higher powers of creativity than mankind has ever accumulated before. And therefore, you want to see an agreement of mankind, as mankind, with no difference in terms of quality.

And our object is, is for mankind, when it comes to physical science, physical scientific discovery; well, physical scientific discovery does not have a language difference inherently, not when it's creativity. And therefore, what we want to do is use the weak powers we have, by special languages, and develop the process of languages, so that mankind in general achieves a degree of creativity, as such, pure human creativity, without any division in anything in anything else. Yes, we recognize what the history of mankind is, the culture of mankind, we recognize all that. But where is it going? Is it going to be stagnant? Is it going to be fixed permanently? For life? No!

What we're trying to do is create a society, on Earth,—ah! But not just on Earth. We're already going into the Galaxy. We are intending to go to the Galaxy, where most of the water that mankind depends upon, will come from! And some people are working on this.

NASA-TV

Mankind is not divided into special cultures: Here a crew of American, Russian, and European origin after their arrival at the International Space Station on March 27, 2015.

Many other important discoveries are emerging in that way.

Mankind is converging on the unity of mankind. The childhood of mankind is changing. Mankind must, and can, grow up. [applause]

Q: [John Sigerson] Hello, Lyn, I think you know me!

LaRouche: I think so!

Q: [follow-up] This bears directly on what you just brought up in terms of unifying culture. But let me back up just a second, to say that over the next few months, we are going to be celebrating two pairs of great musical geniuses: The first pair is J.S. Bach and Handel, who are contemporaries. Tomorrow, we are going to be celebrating J.S. Bach in an extension of Manhattan, namely, Brooklyn; and with a performance of the *Jesu, meine Freude*. And then in December, we are going to be celebrating Handel with a doubleheader performance of the Handel *Messiah*.

But I want to focus in on the other pair that I have a question for you about. The first of those is Schubert, Franz Schubert. Just yesterday, we began the process of working through the famous Schubert *Schwanengesang, The Swan Song*—his incredible posthumous settings of two wonderful poets in German—and we will be presenting those next month at a Musikabend, with two tenors and one baritone; it's unfortunately not three tenors. [laughter] But we will be presenting that.

Ideas vs. 'Talk-Talk'

And then, something you may not know,—but in the late winter or early spring, we will have the opportunity to perform Verdi,—choral works by Verdi, in a church where the organ will have been tuned to the Verdi tuning, which is a real first in Manhattan; I think it's probably a real first in the United States, maybe a real first in the world!

So my question bears on the two types of singing, and the two mindsets of singing Schubert and singing Verdi. These two ways of singing or ways of thinking, tend to be divergent in terms of their overall approach; and many singers specialize in the one and the other.

But thinking about what you just said, what I'm searching for, is a means of integrating the emotional intensity, intimate intensity, of the Schubert *Lied*, and the *Lieder* from other great *Lieder* composers, like Schumann and Brahms; with the grandeur, the dramatic grandeur of a Verdi. Which also bears on bridging the gap between and the remainders of the gap between the great Italian vocal culture, and the great German vocal culture. And I'm trying to find a way to go in the direction that you just said, in terms of *one* culture: How do we do that? How do we see that way?

LaRouche: I think it's a natural thing to do, and I think the problem is that there's been a division in opinion on these things, which should not be, there should be unification. And we're doing it, we're raising it right now. What we're doing in this Manhattan and related areas, is exactly what we should be doing. Because we have to understand that there is no such thing as a language, *per se.* And when you get into the area of Classical musical composition and its performance, you get into that area: Suddenly, you are in an area where you're no longer using speech as such, or what we use as speech. It becomes something—a different thing.

And I think that Verdi, of course, is typical of this, but there are other things, that are also the same thing from Bach on. Because Bach actually gained a great creative process, and then other people began to do things. And Schubert has very specific differences we can all know. If we know Schubert's compositions at all, we know what the difference is! And we know what the importance of that difference is.

So, what we need is to understand, is that we're not using simple talking language. Talk-talk language! That is not the way to understand the human mind. You should know that on every street corner; what do you get? Talk-talk-talk! Where's your music? Where's the beauty? Where's the meaning of the idea? Where's the meaning of ideas?

And what is the importance of Verdi, for example? Now Verdi is something which I had a lot of fun with, over much of my life. I had less experience with it in these years, than I had in my youthful years, but so be it. But nonetheless, the fact is that music, and the drama that goes with music and things that also correlate with the same thing, have the same thing: *They are not the spoken language!* The spoken language will get you almost nowhere. And often it will tend to do so more often than not.

The idea of what we call music, which has an extension into other expressions, is peculiar to what we call the artistic mode. And the artistic mode is the truest ex-

The concluding scene from Giuseppe Verdi's opera La Traviata.

Washington National Opera

pression of the intention of mankind. And what we try to do, is we try not to go backward in terms of those kinds of conceptions and progress,—but we have to realize that we have to look forward to what we have not yet discovered in this direction. But the first thing to do, is to take the idea of music, as it's properly performed and used, and that's a point of reference,—but that's not the end of it. We have to go to areas which we have not yet gone to. And it will be a consequence of what has been done with great music now. [applause]

Q: Hi, I'm D—, I currently come from Washington, D.C. area. This week in Washington, the biggest thing is of course the Benghazi hearings with Hillary Clinton, and Obama. From what I gathered, in working where I work, that of course there's the [tussle] between the Democrats and the Republicans, like a showdown. My biggest question is how's it going to impact Hillary and Obama at this point, and how soon can we expect Hillary to drop her Presidential campaign after all of this?

The Problem of Africa
LaRouche: I think the first thing, is Hillary has to be dumped. There's no question about that. I mean, she lies too much, among other things, and that's not a good thing. So she lies. And actually, she's a stooge of Obama. She was intimidated by his presence; she was also pragmatic in terms of the way she behaved; and

what she has done is she has destroyed anything which had been respectable about her! She has destroyed herself!

And we have some other people who are running for President, and they are also not fit for human beings, human usage. And therefore we have to consolidate ourselves on that.

And this all goes to the same thing; we just got through it, what John represented. You have to realize: what's the importance, of Classical artistic composition? Why is it different than the spoken language in ordinary ways? What's wrong with that? hmm? In other words, why is artistic composition absolutely essential? Why is it the fact that this does not match with ordinary spoken words? It doesn't. Ordinary spoken words don't mean much; they are simply a trash basket, that enable you to grunt and whine, and so forth, hmm?

What we call music, when we're talking seriously about music,—we're talking about mankind's going into a deeper form of knowledge, quality of knowledge; of man's knowledge which is the knowledge, of creativity. And the function of artistic composition, is that it is the standard which defines the meaning of human. And as human is not done in words, as such, it's not done in so-called practice, popular practice; it's done by the art of creativity, the creativity that goes with Classical artistic composition in all forms: in painting, different kinds of art,—all these things, why do they exist? Why should they exist? Because you have to go outside the common use of words and gestures, if you want to find out the meaning of human life. And that's what it's all about.

Q: Good afternoon, Mr. LaRouche, how are you today? I'm E—.

LaRouche: I am not in good condition, but I'm functioning.

Q: [follow-up] OK, wonderful. I went to Washington on Wednesday [for the Day of Action], and it was very good. I realize that we used charm and good humor, and some of the aides in the offices of the Representatives, they were very receptive. And we went to different offices, and left the literature, so I think we are making headway.

Now, yesterday, I went a little later than everyone else, to the function on 45th St., because I said, it's best to deal with politicians after they have drunk [laughter]—alcohol. I spoke to a gentleman; he was from Local 79. So he said, "Oh! I know you, I know LaRouche. I hope he is not running for President again, because he's splitting the votes. He wants the Republicans to win." I said, "C'mon! that is not like that! He wants to promote Glass-Steagall, so you can have more for your men working." So, we talked about different things.

A genocidal travesty: Teaching Rwandans how to install solar panels at health clinics, rather than providing a modern electrical grid.

However, I waited until Senator Schumer came out. I said, "Hello, Senator Schumer, thank you for responding to my letters, when they did not pass the extension." So, I said, "Right now, I'm an activist in the LaRouche PAC, and we are pushing Glass-Steagall." He said, to let you know that he is on your side. [laughter]

LaRouche: Well, that's nice!

Q: [follow-up] Yes. So, I spoke to another lady; she is a Senator for New York State, so I let her know, "Listen: You need to develop a little bit more balls than the men, because they're not really looking out for the women." [laughter] I think she was embarrassed, but I said, "Listen, you know what? You have to be a pit bull; you cannot allow these men to really dictate to you, and they're not doing anything much." So she was happy to hear that, but I think she was nervous.

One other thing. I must say, I've been sending emails to different people. And I got a response from a friend of mine who doesn't know much; in school, he was the biggest dunce, and I think right now, he still is, but he has money. He let me know he is not proud of me, because I am trying to unseat Obama. You know, I said, "thank you for your response," but I will deal with him after he is like a little calmer. I think at least 90% of the people, they're sleeping; they do not know what is really going on.

And certain things always bother me: in terms of

Africa, three-quarters of the country is there for the protection of animals, where the people cannot plant. But I was reading certain information, and I said: "Oh, now I know why it is like this: because if people cannot plant, they have to rely on the government or some aid from America or some other country." And I think the land should be given back to the people, so they can cultivate it, instead of having three-eighths of a country allocated to the animals, instead of the population. And that has been happening a lot in Africa, especially under the British rule.

So what do you think?

The CO$_2$ Hoax

LaRouche: I think that Obama is a disaster for everybody, including himself. But he's not curable, that's the only difference; other people are able to cure themselves. Obama is not able to cure himself, and that's his tragedy.

But the problem is,—the Africa thing? I know very well. Not completely, but I've had some experiences in that area, and I know what goes on in that area. And this is something that's a saddening experience there. And nothing has been done, much, to solve this problem.

But this is evil; my view of it, is it's purely evil, what's happened. And you see what's happened with Obama. Obama is typical of evil. He represents nothing but evil. And his stepfather was also evil, and the policy of the Obama administration is evil; it's explicitly evil.

And it's not something which you can say is "also evil." No. It *is* evil. And Obama's evil. And what he's doing in killing people all over the planet now, and so forth. We have to get rid of it! We have to have the law come in, and say, "No, you don't do this any more."

And everything that's wrong with Africa, is a result of what was done against Africa! And that's the point. And we should all be able, who know anything about anything, should know that that's the case. The problem is the history of Africa is that it was one of the areas that was a target area, as much as anything else. And it has to be ended. And some people in Africa have tried to do that, and I think they've had some progress in it. But the problems we also know,—the thing that's conspicuous to us, is the fact that we see the shame of what is done in Africa, inside Africa, and that angers me.

Speed: I want to bring somebody to the microphone now, who I want to do a little introduction of. Lyn, Tom Wysmuller has come. He is the gentleman who helped us do our press conference a couple of weeks ago, back at the United Nations.

And as he comes to the microphone, let me just say, we are engaged in a war, thanks to Mr. LaRouche, not with words and the kind of weapons that are being used in this global warming hoax, but with a polemic to destroy the high priesthood of Newtonian science, so-called, pseudo-science; and Tom has been in the ranks doing that. So, Tom, why don't you say what you got to say? [*applause*]

Tom Wysmuller: Thank you for having me here. I mean, in all honesty, you ought to applaud *after* I say what I'm saying. [laughter]

I think I can tie together the last three speakers and what I want to talk about, all in one wrap. I'm going to talk about sea level and CO_2. Now, I'm in a room of humanists here, people who are embodying what we need to expand the human spirit. So, why are CO_2 and sea level connected? Well, I'm going to try to explain it, and I'm going to try to do it as quickly as I can.

Most of you have this handout, looks like this, and I'm not going to read it, but I'm going to describe the gist of what's in here. Because what's happened in the last 130 years or so, CO_2 has skyrocketed, from a level 280 parts per million [ppm] for 2,000 years, and all of a sudden, as the industrial age begins, it shoots up!

Well, something didn't shoot up. And what didn't shoot up, was sea level in those areas in the world which are, and I'm going to define this, tectonically inert. And "tectonically inert" means places that are neither rising nor falling. Nor, Norway had an enormous load of ice during the last Ice Age. When the ice melted the pressure was off, and Norway rose. On the other side, Holland and Belgium sunk, like a see-saw. In between the two is a place called Wismar, Germany: and Wismar doesn't sink and doesn't rise. And the sea level has a slow, steady rise, due to the thermal expansion of the oceans. The problem, is CO_2 has skyrocketed—and there is *no* acceleration whatsoever, in those places on Earth that are tectonically inert. So that connection between sea level and CO_2, just isn't there.

Governor Jerry Brown

Now, how does this connect to all the other stuff? Well, in Paris in a few weeks, they're going to try to talk and convince the nations of the world, to spend *billions* of dollars, and euros, and yen, and renminbi, to combat sea-level rise due to CO_2. It is a fraud! Where you want to spend the money, and this is where I can tie into the other speakers: Africa can be electrified for a *tenth* of what you're trying to spend, to quote "combat CO_2," which happens to be a life-giving gas for plants. The *entire continent* can be electrified! That means people don't have to go into the forests and gather wood for a few hours a day, so they can boil the water, so they don't get river blindness when they drink it.

And the children who do it, can be in school. *They're* they ones who could be discovering cures for cancer, ways to connect the music of Schubert and Brahms, and all the other things that we talk about, the higher things that human beings can do. But if they're on a subsistence economy, they cannot do it.

And if you keep them, and spend that money and waste it down a rat-hole, which is where they want to send it, those people will never see electricity; they'll never be able to contribute to humanity,—and you can add South America, India, and Indonesia to that, too. And there's enough money for all of it, if they don't waste it on combatting CO_2.

So that is my plea to you: If you can spread that word, and send this to every embassy, consulate of every Third World country, Second World country, and First World country, so they get it, before they go to Paris. [applause]

LaRouche: Oh, thank you, Tom. This was as energetic as you did before, in your earlier period before. But the point is, we have to recognize the fact that the whole thing that we are dealing with is one gigantic fraud. And I think you told that story in the earlier period, and I think it stands up today right now: that this whole thing is a fraud. And the whole policy is a fraud. It's entirely a fraud!

We have the governor of California is a fraudster. He's really one of the leading fraudsters on the planet. Others we'll come across will also do something similar, but right now, he's put himself out in front, as the biggest faker on the planet in terms of this science.

Wysmuller: Well, I'm energetic about it, because I really believe in this, and I want to get that message out as best as I can.

LaRouche: Excellent!

Mankind will Control the Solar System

Q: Good afternoon, Lyndon LaRouche! We're calling Manhattan "the Land of Hamilton and LaRouche" these days, and we're driving the British banksters out. We've had a terrific amount of fun doing that,

All this week, there have been squads of younger and older generations of your movement here, resonating against the British invasion, which you drew attention to immediately after that devastating debacle, the so-called Democratic Presidential debates there was suddenly an emergence of all kinds of British Barons and Tim Geithner himself dared to come out, under the guise of a Baruch College economics seminar; and it was absolutely disgraceful! There were almost 1,000 people who attended, but the only way they could get them there, was in the cloak of darkness. They turned out the lights, they had security better than O'Hare Airport; no one could get in that wasn't vetted. You had to sign up online, and there could have been nothing but a bunch of spooks there; it was sort of a pre-Hallowe'en event.

But we broke it up by simply saying,—when Mr. Geithner was saying, "I knew of no model, there was nothing we could do, there was no model." And so I had to protest: "There is a model, and you know it well, Mr. Geithner. FDR used this model and put millions of Americans to work, and put the bankers in jail. It's called Glass-Steagall. And we're going to get it through the House and the Senate, and you're going to jail." It was quite effective in breaking up the controlled environment.

So we're going to keep that edge going, and the British will be gone, and Glass-Steagall will be imple-

mented if we have anything to do about it.

LaRouche: Well, "begone," is a good term. The term is "begone," or "be gone." It's a good term to use.

Q: Good afternoon, Mr. LaRouche. I have a question about the environment, about what our guest was talking about. In view of the amount of propaganda in the media, and even in commercial advertising about global warming, how can we best use what resources we have to fight this global warming and alleged CO_2 buildup?

LaRouche: I think there is no such thing as this warming thing. I think it's a fraud completely. The point is, mankind has to actually define ways in which to regulate the environment: Mankind must regulate the environment! Now we only hope that mankind will do it competently and not incompetently. That's all there is to it.

The history of mankind,—look, mankind is a creative species, like no other species we know of. And all the peculiarities of mankind, those which are good, are man-made! Mankind is the source of creativity which enables mankind, to develop the planet. But it's not just the planet. The Galactic System is there; and the Galactic System is not just one Galaxy, it's a nest of galaxies. The water system on Earth depends upon the Galactic System; your water depends upon the Galactic System and the management of it. And its management is what's important. And the management is provided by what? It's provided chiefly by mankind.

Only mankind has the ability to create a change in its own existence, by making what are tantamount to improvements in mankind's ability to deal with things. And this goes with the Galaxy; it goes with the Galactic System. It's not just what happens on Earth. Mankind has an impact beyond Earth! That's the essence. The development of mankind's skills, the development of all the things that mankind developed, the achievements are all of that nature.

Now, people try to pick it out and say, "explain this, this is this, this guy did this," but that's not what happened. What happened was that mankind has been developed, and is developed, to create new forms of organization of the Solar System and beyond! And because we're now getting close to the "beyond" question, much more than before.

So it wasn't just a landing on Mars, but landing on Mars is a warning sign that mankind is going to control the Solar System, and mankind is also,—as we find when we look at the Galaxy, mankind is also a process characteristic of the whole system.

So therefore, these are the kinds of things which we can know, which are little discussed, which are little examined; but we know from what we know so far, that that's the case. Mankind is not only what you call him to be, but mankind is the *creative force*. We will find out in the course of subsequent history, we're going to find out how powerful mankind is, within and beyond the Solar System.

We have yet to understand the majesty of that conception. But somebody else will, hopefully, make that point clear. And what we just raised,—you know, what he raised on this thing is the same kind of thing. You have to have a very careful consideration of the processes on which mankind's existence depends, and you have to understand how you can do something good, to help maintain those processes.

And keep all the screwballs out from making a mess of the thing! That's the other side of the thing.

But you have to have, first of all, a conception of what the principle is; and secondly, we have to get rid of the screwballs who have these great recipes.

Speed: This will be our final question for today.

Q: Good afternoon, Mr. LaRouche, D—. I have a problem that people have their own lives, and [how] to go ahead and get them to think outside of their own lives, with the propaganda that's been given out. Goebbels must have done a beautiful job here, even though

Only mankind has the ability to create a change in its own existence, by making what are tantamount to improvements in mankind's ability to deal with things. And this goes with the Galaxy; it goes with the Galactic System. It's not just what happens on Earth. Mankind has an impact beyond Earth! That's the essence. The development of mankind's skills, the development of all the things that mankind developed, the achievements are all of that nature.

NASA

The Hubble telescope shows a starburst ring around Galaxy Messier 94.

he's dead!

The idea is to go ahead and get people to get our ideas out and to accept them, when they have their own little lives to go ahead and organize within.

LaRouche: OK, good. I got the gist of that.

Speed: OK, Lyn, that's everything for day. I just want to invite you now to conclude, and we'll get to work.

LaRouche: Have some fun! [applause]

Every Day Counts In Today's Showdown To Save Civilization

That's why you need EIR's **Daily Alert Service**, a strategic overview compiled with the input of Lyndon LaRouche, and delivered to your email 5 days a week.

For example: On Sept. 30 EIR's Daily Alert featured Lyndon LaRouche's warning that the action must be taken immediately to remove President Obama in order to not only avoid further provocations toward World War III, but to avoid a disorderly collapse of Wall Street.

"If Wall Street collapses in a debt panic, that chaotic destructive force can lead to death and destruction in the United States and around the world," he said. FDR's Glass-Steagall is needed now.

Russian President Vladimir Putin's recent initiative in Syria has weakened Obama and created the necessary opening to do what's needed. But time is of the essence.

This is intelligence you need to act on, if we are going to survive as a nation and a species. Can you really afford to be without it?

THURSDAY, OCTOBER 1, 2015

EIR Daily Alert Service

EIR DAILY ALERT SERVICE P.O. BOX 17390, WASHINGTON, DC 20041-0390

- LaRouche: Wall Street Must Be Shut Down Before It Crashes
- Kerry Confirms Shift in U.S. Policy on Syria, Assad
- Putin Orders First Air Strikes Against Syrian Jihadists
- Russia's Upper House Approves Use of Armed Forces Abroad
- German Government Rejects Turkish Proposal for 'Safe Zones' in Syria
- Senator Warren: Glass-Steagall 'Is Exactly What We Should Do'
- German Saving Banks Threatened by Zero Rates Policy and EU Over-Regulation
- Senator Feinstein Thinks Russia's Move in Syria May Be Positive
- Dana Rohrabacher, Chair, House Subcommittee on Europe, Eurasia, and Emerging Threats, Holds Hearing on Terrorist Threat in Russia
- Rep. Dana Rohrabacher Attacks U.S. Support of Saudis, and Campaign To Overthrow Assad in House Foreign Affairs Committee
- BRICS Foreign Ministers Meet in New York
- NASA May Join Chinese/European Space Science Mission
- Finding Water on Mars Provokes Broad Debate in China
- Secretary John Kerry Reviews the 2013 Powerful Example of Cooperating with

---

International Forum in China Focusses On Women, Development, Future

by Helga Zepp-LaRouche

Oct. 28—On Sept. 27, 2015, Chinese President Xi Jinping delivered a major speech at the Global Leaders Meeting on Gender Equality and Womens Empowerment at the UN in New York, commemorating both the 70th anniversary of the founding of the United Nations as well as the 20th anniversary of the Beijing conference on women. In addition, Chinese First Lady Peng Liyuan addressed the issue of education and women in a subsequent very moving speech at the UN, where she emphasized the enormous progress which has been made in China in this respect, and of which she herself had been a beneficiary, having become a professional soprano and music professor.

The same issue of gender equality and the empowerment of women was the subject of an international conference October 14-16 in Beijing, organized by the Soong Ching Ling Foundation. This Foundation upholds the life and work of the wife of Sun Yat-sen, the founder of modern China; Soong Ching Ling herself was one of the outstanding women of the Twentieth Century and played a role in China comparable to the role Eleanor Roosevelt played for the United States. The Foundation is involved in numerous projects both in China, as well as internationally, focusing on the education and furthering the advancement of girls and women, among many other cultural activities.

The Forum brought together an impressive selection of engaged women from academia, business, social organizations, and politics, who, during the two day conference, highlighted the state of affairs and future perspectives concerning the status of women in many parts of the world. In China, where legislation garantees women equal status, women in urban areas have reached that equality to a very high degree, while in rural areas there are still major gaps, which were mostly attributed to the need for more economic development in those regions.

The speeches reflected a broad array of topics, such as the income gap, social security, legal foundations, leadership training, scientific programms, financial literacy, food security, the role of women in Chinese history, and many more. A European business executive recounted her experience in the world of commerce in different countries, which highlighted, that gender equal-

Peng Liyuan, wife of President Xi Jinping, addresses the United Nations on Sept. 17, 2015.

ity is still far from beeing a reality in the western world.

Most fascinating was the report of a male professor, who described studies about decision-making and the differences between male and female decesion making. Female executives, according to this univerity survey, were found to be more considerate, taking into account more the interest of other people, and ably to see through ambiguities, and in general making fewer mistakes than their more pushy male counterparts. This author was one of the keynote speakers in the opening session of the conference, delivering a speech with the title: Creativity as the true identity of women.

It is very clear, that while parts of China are still in the status of a developing country, and therefore women still have all the known double burdens of child rearing and work, the fact that China has lifted 600 million of its citizens out of poverty in a very short time, has given tremendous chances for women to realize their potential. The extraodinary importance that President Xi Jinping puts on excellence in education, on scientific innovation, and on Confucian values of morality, means that the perspective of gender equality has a better prospect in China today than in most of the western world, where most women have actually internalized a role defined by men in one way or another, and leading women too often to try to prove their leadership by outdoing the men in toughness, and thus loosing the grace and creativity of their gender.

Creativity as the True Identity of Women

by Helga Zepp-LaRouche

As the recent White Paper on the status of women in China emphasizes, great progress has been made boosting gender equality in the last twenty years in the context of the general economic progress made in China. In several categories China has achieved the United Nations Millennium Goals ahead of time.

It is also clear that the gap between the significant progress made in urban centers as compared to the rural areas, which results in the differences in the living standard and educational level between the two areas, is also reflected in the gender issue, and needs further improvement.

But it can be said clearly that the absolute priority and focus the Chinese government has put on education in general, education of girls and women specifi-

Soong Ching Ling (1893-1981), the second wife of the founder of the Chinese Republic, Sun Yat-sen.

cally, and on excellence in education in particular, means that China is one of the trend-setting countries of the world, and may be the most important one.

Very recently, Chinese First Lady, Peng Liyuan, gave a beautiful speech at the United Nations, in English, where she emphasized the importance of girls going to school, since they are the first teachers of their children and therefore impact the next generation; and also the importance of their university education, since education is followed by equality. She said that her Chinese dream is that all children and every young woman on this planet will have access to good education! I know Madam Soong Ching Ling would be extremely happy about this!

I am proud to say it is also my dream. I have said many times that I want to live to see in my lifetime, that every child on this planet has access to universal education, because once that is accomplished, it will be a game-changer, in the sense that the old oligarchical system will be overcome forever. Because oligarchical rule was based on the idea that there would be a small power elite, whose rule depended on the backwardness of the population. Therefore, if every child on the planet has access to universal education, a new epoch of human history will begin, where the creative potential of the human species will be unleashed in ways totally unimaginable today.

True Equality: Ennoble the Individual

While it is indispensable to support gender equality in education through legislation, true equality can only be accomplished when both genders define their actual identity by developing the fullest creative potential embedded in them. Such legislation should therefore be complemented through reflection on an emphasis made by the German poet Friedrich Schiller, after whom the Schiller Institute is named.

Schiller described the female gender as the more aesthetical of the two sexes. Why is this important? After the French Revolution had been taken over by the

Jacobin terror, he wrote the *Aesthetical Letters* as an answer to that failed possibility to replicate the American Revolution in Europe. He said with regret that the objective conditions for change had existed, but that the subjective, the moral preconditions to accomplish that change had been lacking.

From now on, he concluded, every improvement in the political arena would only be possible through the enoblement of the individual, and in order to accomplish that, aesthetical education, especially through great Classical art, had to be emphasized. For the he underlined the development of what is called *Empfindungsvermögen* in German, (for which the English word "sensitivity" is an imperfect translation, and which is closest to *gaushouxing* in Chinese, which means the "quality of being sensitive") to be the most important requirement of his time.

Because that *Empfindungsvermögen*, this emotional and intellectual capability to totally absorb and have empathy with the world, is the key to the subjective moral improvement which enables the individual to act as a world historical individual when the moment of challenge comes, as a representative of the future better era of human history.

Schiller says the female gender has naturally a greater affinity to beauty, and should be called "the beautiful gender," not so much because of its outer beauty, which he calls "architectonic beauty"—which is a gift of nature but not the accomplishment of the person, as differentiated from the beauty of the soul—but because of the response of

Jeanne d'Arc (1412-1431) in a miniature done in the Fifteenth Century.

Marie Curie (1867-1934), the Polish-French scientist who pioneered work in radioactivity.

women to beauty. This is very important because, given the supposed contradiction between reason and the senses, and their corresponding emotions, according to Schiller, beauty is the realm where reason and the senses coincide; in the realm of the senses beauty corresponds to reason.

According to Schiller, among all inclinations which derive from the sensation of beauty and which are the property of fine souls, none appeals more to the moral requirement than the ennobling affection of love, and none produces dispositions which correspond more to the true dignity of the human person. So while the human aspiration to constantly perfect insights into the cognition of true universal principles, and to act on the basis of that cognition, is the same for men and women, it is the greater affinity of women to the Beautiful, and the associated feeling of love, which enables them to play a more important role in the area of the aesthetical education of society. That is, provided they are inner-directed and truth-seeking.

Schiller says, and I agree with him, that the male puts up with an insult to his taste, as long as the inner content of a matter satisfies his mind. Usually he even appreciates it all the more if the essence of the matter emerges more firmly, and the essential is separated from the outer appearance. But the female doesn't forgive the neglected appearance; even if the content is rich, she demands that the form in which that content appears correspond to that richness, and that an outward appearance which does not fulfill the requirements of the aesthetical sen-

Clara Schumann (1819-1896), composer and pianist.

Hawkins Studio, Tuskegee, Al.

Amelia Boynton Robinson (1905-2015), known widely as the Mother of the Civil Rights Movement.

creative commons/Tksteven

Liu Yang (1978-), the first Chinese woman in space.

sation, or even insults it, will be rejected, or at least devalued.

Those women in Western culture who try to counter the male chauvinist dominance of a patriarchical culture by being more manly than man, by trying to imitate all attitudes of the so-called alpha-types of men, are doing neither society nor themselves a favor. (Indeed, as some examples of this type of women in certain Western capitals demonstrate, they tend to be even scarier that their male equivalents.) Nor do those women who put all their emphasis on their outer beauty and appeal, contribute anything valid to the improvement of society.

If, however, the woman is guided by an inner-directed zeal for the development of her own creative powers, her desire to contribute something new to the body of knowledge presently available to mankind, then her

Sister Juana Inés de la Cruz (1651-1695), a self-taught scholar and poet, and nun in Mexico.

greater affinity to beauty adds grace to every undertaking, and succeeds in putting her contemporaries in a positive frame of mind, making their souls more receptive to receiving the truth.

Follow Oustanding Role Models

While the present condition of most areas of the world is yet very far from that ideal,—whether because of the still-existing poverty of billions of people who are forced to focus all their efforts on just providing for their survival and that of their families, or whether it is because of the degradation and decadence of much of present-day Western culture,—it is nevertheless extremely important that outstanding role models such as Jeanne d'Arc, Juana Ines de la Cruz, Marie Curie, Clara Schumann, Soong Ching Ling, Amelia Boynton Robinson, Valentina Tereshkova, or Liu Yang, the famous

Indian Prime Minister Indira Gandhi (1917-1984) at the National Press Club in Washington, D.C. in July 1982.

cosmonaut and taikonaut, inspire present and future generations.

The image of man which was so beautifully developed by such great thinkers and poets as Confucius, Friedrich Schiller, and Wilhelm von Humboldt, shows that the human being is capable of limitless self-perfection, of the harmonious development of all talents embodied in his or her mind, and of the development of a beautiful soul. Schiller defines the beautiful soul as that person for whom freedom and necessity, duty and passion, are one. The only person who fulfills that precondition is a genius,—it's not a utopian fantasy, but a condition which can be reached in reality.

Mankind Must Decide

Mankind is now at a crossroads; we could destroy our species, if we allow geopolitical interests to lead to a new, this time thermonuclear, war, or we can overcome geopolitics by establishing a new paradigm defined by the common aims of mankind, as it is now being expressed, for example, by the win-win strategy of President Xi Jinping. If we reach that second happier possibility, then the true character of makind as the only creative species known so far in the universe, will manifest itself.

We are indeed at a crossroads. The potential for the future is already in motion. The "win-win" model of a new type of relationship among nations, and the type of alternative economic system, as it is coming into being with the BRICS through new financial institutions such as the Asia Infrastructure Investment Bank, the New Development Bank, and other institutions, already represents a perspective of hope.

But it is also a period of extraordinary challenges. Just think of the wars, based on lies, which are now tearing apart the entire region of Soutwest Asia, and think of the terrible effect this has on women in most of Southwest Asia, where many of them are denied the human right of being treated as a human being.

The resulting refugee crisis is tearing apart Europe right now, as millions and millions of people are running away from these wars in the Middle and Near East. But at this moment it is important to remember that women in moments of extraordinary crisis have shown, again and again, extraordinary leadership qualities.

Think, for example, of the women in Germany in the period after the Second World War, who played an absolutely crucial role in rebuilding Germany out of a rubble field. Or think of the many women in Africa, who are fighting for the lives of their children under totally impossible conditions.

Soong Ching Ling said that the condition of women in society is a measure of the development of that nation. And by that yardstick, I can say, no country on the planet is fully developed.

Women in crises often act as heroines, and in light of that, and the special aesthetical talents of women, I want to emphasize that women will have to play the key role in bringing about a cultural renaissance at this time. In the fight for the liberation of women, Soong Ching Ling said: "Join efforts with women around the world, and form a women's United Front."

Because we are faced with the challenges of the world today, I would like to ask that we build such a United Front in her spirit—to establish a just New World Economic Order which will be the absolute precondition for true gender equality. Let's work together to extend the "win-win" perspective for the entire planet!

Thank you.

Germany Can Make History: The Decision for War or Peace

by Helga Zepp-LaRouche

Oct. 23—In the present historical period—in which virtually all seemingly reliable assumptions about society are becoming obsolete, and everyone senses that we are faced with the heavy issues of war and peace, of 'to be or not to be,' of collapse into chaos or a new Classical Renaissance—Germany is one of the few actors on the grand stage of world politics that can help determine which of the two alternatives comes to pass.

So far very few people in Germany think so, but that does not diminish the truth of this statement. Of course, the world-historical role of China is more obvious, and with President Xi Jinping's "win-win" vision of the global expansion of the New Silk Road, China has put a completely new model of relations among nations on the agenda. That model shows, for the first time in history, how the ominous geopolitics that led to two world wars in the Twentieth Century can be overcome—through the cooperation of nations for the common good.

And equally obvious is the importance of the role of Russia—with its strategic partnership with China and its military flank in Syria—which has led to a new balance of forces in the world; that exposes just how hollow the Obama Administration's claim to be the One World Superpower has become.

President Putin has just pointed out—in his speech at this year's meeting of the Valdai Club on the theme of "War and Peace"—the danger that arises if the United States attempts to use its missile defense system in Eastern Europe for a so-called disarming first strike with very precise, modernized nuclear weapons. The intention would be to shift the strategic balance in its favor and dictate its will to the whole world. But such an approach could only lead to mutually assured destruction, Putin said. After the successful nuclear agreement with Iran,

the pretext of an alleged threat of Iranian missiles can no longer be maintained, although the threat never really existed anyway. So why is the missile defense system still being maintained, he asked.

Putin—whose own military operations in Syria against ISIS and other terrorists are successfully advancing step by step—used the same speech to point out the reason for the comparative failure of the American military operation in the region. It is an insoluble contradiction, he said, if you intend to fight the terrorists on the one hand, and on the other, you arm them so that you can overthrow legitimate governments with their help.

No one should miss the delightfully ironic skit on the theme of the confusion of U.S. policy on terrorism in the Middle East in the latest satirical program, "Die Anstalt," based on the schmaltzy show "Blind Date."

Obviously, the American population itself—perhaps

Xinhua/Liu Weibing

Will Germany pursue this option? Chancellor Angela Merkel meets with Chinese President Xi Jinping in Beijing on July 7, 2014.

the most important actor on that world stage—has the responsibility to end and take action against the incessant violations of international law, which have unfortunately become the rule as a result of the continuity of neo-con policies from Bush/Cheney, to today's Obama Administration. These violations range from the wars in Southwest Asia—which were built on lies; to the deployment of drones against alleged terrorists—without any due process of law; or the notorious "collateral damage," which, according to the revelations of the recent whistleblowers to the website *The Intercept*, concerns innocent civilians in over 90% of the cases.

UNHCR/M. Henley

Syrian children sporting the blankets provided by Austrian volunteers, as they wait for transport into Austria, and then on to Germany.

The Congressional investigation now urgently demanded by several organizations could lead very quickly to the impeachment of President Obama, who, according to published documents, has personally put together the target list every Tuesday. The wave of refugees coming to Europe, and especially Germany, is the result of these wars and drone strikes, which have favored, rather than stemmed, the advance of ISIS.

The Refugee Crisis

But in a certain sense, history has passed the ball into Germany's court precisely because of the refugee crisis.

A large majority of the population, faced with the plight of many desperate people, remains firmly ready to help. But at the latest, since the demonstrations sporting mock guillotines, and the approximately 500—according to the Federal Criminal Police Office—attacks against refugee centers this year, and the attempted murder of the Cologne candidate for Mayor Henriette Reker, it is also clear that the dividing line between "concerned citizens" and rightwing extremists, who do not shrink from using force, has been crossed. What President Putin warned about many months ago—that Western support for Nazi organizations in Ukraine would lead to the expansion of such organizations in many European countries—threatens to come true.

The unspeakable situation of the refugees in Slovenia is only a snapshot of the tragedy unfolding; in recent days, refugees who are too lightly dressed have been rounded up like dangerous criminals, by totally overstretched security forces. Such an approach will do nothing to decrease the wave of refugees. If no solution on a new level is found, the situation in all of Europe will lead in the very short term to an escalation, which could expand into chaos and civil war.

There is a solution for this crisis, but it requires correcting a whole array of axiomatically flawed assumptions behind the policy of the West and Germany in particular, over the last decade. The first obvious implication must be to put an immediate end to the wars started under false pretenses. Germany is to blame not only for allowing the mega-spying of its own citizens through the collaboration between the BND and the NSA, but also by knowingly allowing the Ramstein Military base to be used for drone strikes in Southwest Asia, and by its tacit and partially explicit support for Washington's and London's policy for a unipolar world. Only the refusal to participate in the wars against Iraq under the Schröder government, and against Libya, under the Merkel/Westerwelle government, saved a small part of Germany's honor.

Germany has likewise been complicit in carrying out the decades-long conditionalities policy of the IMF and World Bank against the developing sector, a policy which has prevented any real development while setting up a debt spiral, which has solely served the interests of the financial sector of British empire—for which the term "globalization" is just another expression. If millions of refugees today are fleeing not only from wars started on the basis of lies, but also from poverty and disease—the so-called "economic refugees" from the Balkans, Southern Europe, and Africa—it is because of of this policy.

Social tensions in Germany and all of Europe will intensify to the point of explosion if Germany insists on adhering to the same monetarism which is also applied against Europe, and to German Finance Minister Schäuble's "zero deficit" doctrine—under which for the sake of the chimera of a balanced budget, day-care centers, gymnasiums, education programs, pensions, and so forth must be cut in order to be able to provide for the refugees, which goes together with the brutal austerity policy against Greece and all of Southern Europe.

And there is yet another bad, cherished habit, that Germany must get rid of, if we are to find a solution for this crisis: We must throw the green ideology overboard. And we must reject the notion that we can fob off on the so-called developing countries "sustainable, appropriate" development—in point of fact, no development at all—while at the same time building a new "Limes" wall around "Fortress Europe." We need actual development and reconstruction programs for Africa, Southwest Asia, and the Southern hemisphere, which will overcome poverty and underdevelopment.

Those principles discovered by science and art which are universally valid, are called universal because they also apply to developing countries.

Whether mankind will be able to master the current challenges, will depend upon whether we put into effect a new paradigm, which actualizes the highest expressions of the wonderful multiplicity of cultures and civilizations, which the universal history of mankind has produced. And only if we succeed in bringing about a dialogue between representatives of these high phases of different cultures, will we be able to contrast the grand idea of an international entente among peoples, to the limits of the acountant's mentality or the simple-mindedness of idiots.

If Germany were to say, "We demand that these wars stop; that a real development policy combined with that of the BRICS countries for the construction of the World Land Bridge be put on the agenda; that we immediately integrate the refugees, but at the same time develop their homelands with the construction of the New Silk Road,"— if we hearken back to our own highest Classical culture, and begin a dialogue of cultures with the highest level of other cultures, then we Germans can make history.

I am optimistic that that can be done.

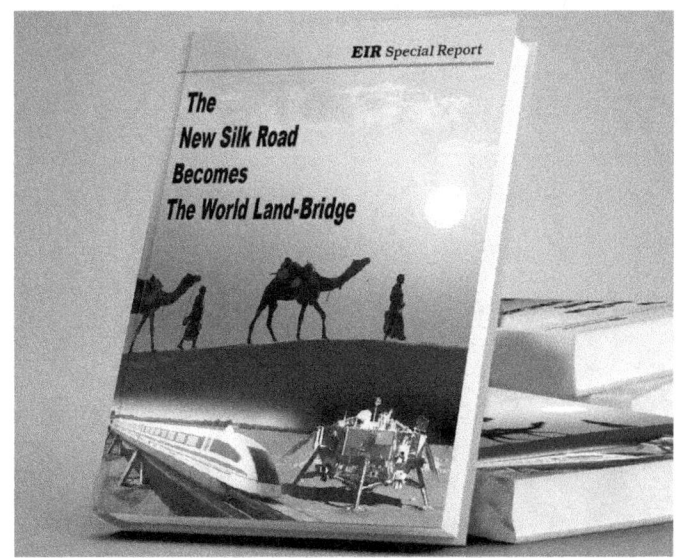